SHINE ON: HOW TO GROW AWESOME INSTEAD OF OLD

CLAIRE COOK

Books by Claire Cook

The Wildwater Walking Club (#1)

The Wildwater Walking Club: Back on Track (#2)

The Wildwater Walking Club: Step by Step (#3)

Time Flies

Wallflower in Bloom

Shine On: How to Grow Awesome Instead of Old

Never Too Late: Your Roadmap to Reinvention

Must Love Dogs (#1)

Must Love Dogs: New Leash on Life (#2)

Must Love Dogs: Fetch You Later (#3)

Must Love Dogs: Bark & Roll Forever (#4)

Must Love Dogs: Who Let the Cats In? (#5)

Must Love Dogs: A Howliday Tail (#6)

Must Love Dogs: Hearts & Barks (#7)

Best Staged Plans

Seven Year Switch

Summer Blowout

Life's a Beach

Multiple Choice

Ready to Fall

Praise for Shine On & Claire Cook

"A veritable fountain of exciting and practical suggestions for women who want to make sure that even though one cannot help growing older, she can indeed keep from growing old."—*Pamela Kramer, Examiner*

"I highly recommend this new book. You're never too old to get started!"—*Sharon's Garden of Book Reviews*

"Full of inspirational quotes as well as practical suggestions, this is a perfect book to begin a new year on the right foot."—*Looking on the Sunnyside*

"Dedicated to "forty-to-forever women," *Shine On* offers sage advice not just on aging well, but living well. With her trademark wit and honesty, Claire Cook covers everything from big picture motivation on following your dreams and remembering to have fun, to practical, hands-on tips on fitness, healthy eating, and her favorite beauty products . . . Claire Cook's wisdom, candor, and effervescent enthusiasm shine on in every word she writes."—*Book Perfume*

"Claire Cook just gets it."—*Meg Cabot*

"Cook's penchant for hitting the emotional sore spot and combining it with humor hits the mark."
—*New York Journal of Books*

"Cook's poignancy and sassy humor resonate with readers; her theme of reinvention uplifts and inspires."—*Savannah Magazine*

"Cook's humor and narrative execution are impeccable."—*Publishers Weekly*

Publisher's Note: This is a work of fiction. Names, characters, places, and incidents are a product of the author's imagination. Locales and public names are sometimes used for atmospheric purposes. Any resemblance to actual people, living of dead, or to businesses, companies, events, institutions, or locales is completely coincidental.

Marshbury Beach Books
Cover Photo: zhuzhu
Shine On/ Claire Cook
ISBN paper 978-1-942671-16-9
ISBN ebook: 978-1-942671-17-6

SHINE ON: HOW TO GROW AWESOME INSTEAD OF OLD

To forty-to-forever women everywhere—
Grow awesome along with me.
The best is yet to be.

As we let our light shine, we unconsciously give other people permission to do the same.

—Marianne Williamson

Flipping the Switch

The thing about life is that it sneaks up on you.

Especially if you're as good at denial as I am.

So there I was, reinvention to the left of me, reinvention to the right of me. Reinvention is the story of my own life. It's my passion, my life's work. I wrote my first novel in my minivan at 45. At 50, I walked the red carpet at the Hollywood premiere of the movie adaptation of my most well known book, *Must Love Dogs*, starring Diane Lane and John Cusack.

I'd gone on to write thirteen novels, turned *Must Love Dogs* into a series. Reinvented my publishing career and become a *New York Times* bestselling author under my own steam. I'd even written my first nonfiction book, *Never Too Late: Your Roadmap to Reinvention (without getting lost along the way)*, to share everything I'd learned on my own reinvention journey that might help other women in theirs.

I was strong. I was invincible. I was—.

Getting older by the nanosecond.

As Dr. Seuss said, "How did it get so late so soon?"

A milestone birthday is on my horizon and I'm not sure

what to make of it. How to deal with it, or even if I want to. What it means. What it could mean.

Further complicating things, if I'm really honest with myself I don't like how I'm feeling physically, not to mention what I see when I forget to look away and accidentally catch myself in the mirror. And given the way the years are flying by, the startling disconnect between who I am on the inside and the stranger I see reflected back at me doesn't seem likely to get better.

And, oh, those existential questions. *Who am I? What am I here for? What do I want my life to be? What do I want to look like?* (Okay, maybe that last one isn't quite existential.) Wouldn't you think we could ask and answer these big questions once, or even twice, in our lifetime and then shift into cruise control?

I'm old enough to know the signs: It's time to get my act together.

Again.

As I ponder some more, I realize that what I really, really want to do is figure out how to grow awesome instead of old. How to shine on, and hopefully on and on and on. And because the comment I hear most often from my readers is, hands down, *Ohmigod, you're writing my life*, I figure that if I'm struggling with all this stuff, I'm not alone.

So let's do this. Let's figure it out together.

Defining Midlife

Just so you know, my definition of midlife is anytime from 40's-on-the-horizon until we die. I have absolutely no intention of ever calling myself part of whatever the next category is. Upper middle age? Lower old age? Endlife?

So for the purposes of this book, and maybe even for the purposes of our lives, let's think of midlife as the forty-to-forever stage.

Location Scouting

I'm picturing us standing at the crossroads of awesome and old. It's not quite as nice a place to be as that corner in Winslow, Arizona made famous by The Eagles in "Take It Easy." A song that, by the way, is now playing nonstop in my head.

Friends of mine once drove cross-country just to stand at that corner, which has been commemorated by Standin' on the Corner Park. Two days later they finally pulled off Route 66, "Take It Easy" blaring, singing along at the top of their lungs, only to find a detour around the legendary spot. They circled around and around, trying unsuccessfully to get closer, which made for an entirely different kind of song. Sheryl Crow's "Detour?" Joni Mitchell's "The Circle Game?"

So if we're going to have an epiphany, or even two or three, as we reinvent our lives to grow awesome instead of old, we should choose our breakthrough locations carefully, right?

I start considering the epic possibilities. I could follow the inspirational breadcrumbs and spend a year in Provence—or more likely six days and five nights if I can find a really good deal. I could eat my way through Italy, meditate my way through India. I could hike the Pacific Crest Trail, at least as far as my fear of heights and my trusty walking sneakers can take me.

I could walk Spain's Camino de Santiago, one of the most famous pilgrimage routes in the world. I once did a book event that included speaking to a large group and having lunch with a smaller gathering of women afterward. One of my luncheon tablemates had just retired after thirty-some years of teaching. She told me that she was leaving the following week to walk "The Camino" with her husband, a longtime dream of theirs. They'd signed up for a tour from Leon to Santiago that would require them to walk five to eight hours a day for two weeks straight.

There was nothing about this woman that exactly screamed fit. "Wow," I said. "Good for you. So what are you doing to get ready for it?"

She rolled her eyes. "You sound just like my husband. He's been training every day for months. I'll be fine. I'll just take my time."

It's been a few years, but right now I imagine heading off to Spain only to find this lovely woman still sitting along the side of the road. Maybe we could walk together.

Instead, I decide that I'm not feeling very epic or high drama right now. I want to make this awesome thing work within the confines of my everyday life. To see if I can figure it out without having to book a flight, pack my bags.

What I really want to do is to find myself without having to lose myself. Or maybe in a way I've already lost myself, so I might as well just cut to the chase and find myself again. Sort of a reinvention staycation, something we can all afford, something that doesn't involve leaving behind our oversize containers of shampoo and conditioner as well as our favorite pillows.

It's official. At least the first leg of this journey needs to happen at home. That way when we *do* decide to go somewhere, we can take our awesomeness with us.

Awesome Sauce

The Oxford Dictionary defines awesome as "extremely impressive or daunting; inspiring great admiration." I start searching for synonyms online, rule out a few old school meanings like fearsome, dreaded and awful, and find lots to like: cool, inspiring, excellent, amazing, awe-inspiring, impressive, magnificent, grand, wondrous, marvelous, mind-blowing, jaw-dropping, formidable, stunning, staggering, terrific, extraordinary, breathtaking, astounding.

I'm feeling the power already. I decide it would be totally awesome to make a little motivational gift for us, a Shine On word cloud we can print out. We can put it anywhere we need inspiration—above our computers, on our refrigerators, over our bathroom mirrors.

Here it is:

How cool is that! It's even shaped like the star we know we are! You can go to ClaireCook.com and print out a larger one. Share it with all your friends. Send it as an ecard. Have it made into a coffee mug. Google up some word cloud sites and design your own. (I used tagul.com.)

I glance at my office clock. In the time it has taken me to figure out how to make us a word cloud shaped like a star, we have both grown an hour and a half older. And the pages I would have finished writing for us by now are still hanging over my head.

It's not that there's anything wrong with word clouds. It's just that making one at this particular time was pure stalling on my part. And even as I type this, I'm resisting the urge to go back online and have my new creation made into a T-shirt so I can parade around my house in it like a midlife Wonder Woman.

I've barely inched my way into this book and already procrastination has jumped out in front of me, waving its arms. *Hey, over here! Look at me!* Staying on the straightaway toward a destination instead of spinning off on an immediate gratification detour will always be a challenge, at least for me. So I do the only thing you can do when these things happen. I shake it off and get back on track.

Quick Suggestion

Okay, so where were we? Right, awesome. As I read through these awesome words again, I realize there's nothing specific about any of them. So in a way we're each going to have to figure out our own personal definition of awesome, come up with our unique recipe for awesome sauce.

As one of my favorite George Carlin bits goes, "I went to a bookstore and asked the saleswoman, 'Where's the self-help section?' She said if she told me, it would defeat the purpose."

All by way of saying my awesome might not be your awesome. Yours might not be mine. But along the way, I think it's really important that we embrace the ideas that work for us without bashing the ones that don't.

We're all different—our beliefs and goals and styles and personalities. If your forehead doesn't wrinkle anymore when you try to raise your eyebrows, and a deep set of parentheses no longer curves from the corners of your nose to the corners of your mouth, that shouldn't make me crazy because Botox and other injectables are not my thing. If I'm a vegetarian, I shouldn't try to make you feel guilty about those barbecued ribs you just chowed down. If your friend finds her inner entrepreneur and launches a booming boomer business, that shouldn't make you feel inadequate because of your choice to add river rafting and more classical music to your life.

Our world has become so polarized that sometimes we need to take a moment to remember that you and your personal choices are not in any way a reflection on my choices and me. When we let go of the judgment and criticism, taking the time to consider other women's decisions can help lead us to our own.

Lots of *Never Too Late* readers have emailed me to say how much another suggestion I offered in that book helped them. So I'm going to repeat it here: If something I say on the pages that follow doesn't resonate for you, ignore it. Maybe you're not there yet. Maybe you have no intention of ever being there. That's okay. Just turn the page and move on.

But if it provokes a strong negative reaction—*that Claire Cook has no idea what she's talking about* or *that's the most ridiculous thing I've ever heard*—or if it just really pisses you off, write it down before you move on. Bookmark it. Highlight it. Mark it with a Post-It.

In a week or two, go back and take another look. Sometimes what we really, really need to hear to get where we're going is the hardest thing to hear, the thing that initially infuriates us the most.

Sharing and Daring

When I started writing my first nonfiction book after all those novels, I honestly didn't know if I could do it. Maybe my brain was permanently set in fiction mode. But then I figured, worse case scenario, if it didn't work out, I could just turn it into a long blog post, or even a couple of Facebook posts and a Tweet or two. And like most things in life, once I stopped worrying about it and jumped in wholeheartedly, I was okay. I hung in there, page after page, day after day, and eventually it turned into a book.

But I have to tell you, I never once imagined I'd write a second nonfiction book. A big part of my decision to write this one came from receiving all those responses to *Never Too Late*. *Thank you for sharing your mistakes so honestly*, many of the readers said in one way or another. *You made me feel so much better about mine.*

Well, I thought, there are certainly more where those came from! Perhaps I did have more to share in the nonfiction realm after all. I mean, if there's one thing I'm consistently brilliant at, it's making mistakes.

The story of my hair reinvention also hit a chord for readers. Many women emailed to say it gave them the courage to embrace their own silver tresses. A few reached out to defend their right to dye. (As if I were some kind of gray hair pusher!)

There were lots of questions, too. *How did I find the time to write so many books? How did I find the courage to try new things? Where did I get my energy? How did I manage to look so good in my photos?* Some of these questions made me laugh—I've certainly had my share of horrifying photos floating around the Internet for all the world to see. But I've also been given some great tips along the way by savvy experts, things I'd be more than happy to share.

What really blew me away was that so many of these messages went on to ask *Do you think I'm too old to try this? Or do that?* One of the women was only 36. Another 43. More were in their 50s and 60s and beyond. It broke my heart that age felt like such an obstacle to them. And it made me think about how easy it is for all of us to fall into the trap of letting our chronological ages define us.

So now what I'm overthinking (another one of my talents!) is that because this book was in part inspired by the response to *Never Too Late*, there's going to be some overlap. I'll do my best to find the balance between making sure both books are freestanding and not getting overly repetitive. In moments of doubt, I've wondered why I didn't have the foresight to envision two books from the beginning. That way I could have saved all the parts that specifically related to growing awesome instead of old for this book.

But here's the thing. If I'd known I was going to someday turn *Must Love Dogs* into a series (four books and counting!), I would have set up the story to make that much easier to do. If I'd known I was going to move from Boston to Atlanta, I wouldn't have bought that last winter coat. Or those cross-country skis, come to think of it. If you knew your marriage wasn't going to last, you might have kept your maiden name so you didn't have to go through the hassle of changing it back, or even stayed in touch with that old boyfriend.

But we can't live our lives like that, always holding back just in case. And I can't write a book that way either. I can't think *Well, that's enough cool stuff for this one—I'll save this character or that topic for the next book.* I can only pour every single thing I can think of, especially my heart and soul, into each book I write to try to make it the best it can be. And trust that by the time the next book rolls around, that proverbial well will fill up with plenty of other cool stuff.

As Anne Lamott said, "If you give freely, there will always be more."

So that's what I did in *Never Too Late*, and what I'll try to do again in *Shine On*. Share every single thing I can think of that might possibly help you on this particular journey.

And if I screw up here and there along the way, I can only hope it will make you feel better about your own mistakes!

First Stop, Fun!

I know, I know. One minute I'm telling you that we have to stay on track and the next I'm saying we're going to start with fun.

But the truth is that I've rarely met a midlife woman, me included, who doesn't need more fun in her life. So while I'm absolutely going to get my daily pages of this book written first thing every day, right after that I'm going to have some fun. And I hope you'll join me.

Okay, so midlife, the forty-to-forever stage. By this point we've been giving and giving for a huge chunk of our lives. We've been focused on our careers and/or our families. If we went the kid route, some of us are squished into the center of a giving sandwich—on the one side we're giving to our growing or teenage or boomeranging kids or to our grandchildren, and on the other side to our increasingly needy parents. Even if our lives are easier in many respects than they were when we were younger, somewhere along the way we've often stopped giving to ourselves.

As my friend Beth said, "I realized I'd forgotten how to play."

So let's learn to play again! Let's have some fun!

When I finally found the courage to write my first novel right before I turned 45, I decided there was enough pain and suffering in the world without me adding to it. I wanted to write the fun books, the books that make women laugh and feel better about their own lives, the ones they'd take with them to read on vacation.

I'm flashing back to a weekly writing group I belonged to in the early days of my career. I'm the newbie of the bunch, and I'm really grateful to have been invited. One week I take my turn reading pages from my book-in-progress while everybody follows along, making notes on the individual printouts I've provided.

It's so hard to put yourself out there like that. My heart is beating double-time and the tremble in my hands matches the one in my voice. As I read, I'm both thrilled and seriously relieved that most of the group members are laughing out loud.

When I finish, I take a deep breath and resist the urge to scrunch my eyes shut while I wait for everybody to give me their verdict.

The writer whose turn it is to critique my pages first has a pretty high opinion of her own importance to the world of literature. I gulp. I'm all too aware that she didn't laugh once as I was reading, so I try to steel myself against whatever is coming.

"Fun appears to be a priority for you," she says, making it sound about as appealing as lint.

Her comment is clearly intended as a put-down, and it hits me between my ribs like a punch. Back then I try to shrug it off so I can take in the rest of her remarks. But in my mind, right now I'm flipping her off like a midlife rebel and saying, "Yes, fun *is* a priority for me. Deal with it."

I think fun should be a priority for all of us. And we don't have to justify it to anyone. Time's a tickin'. Let's get it while we can. And while it's certainly true that there can be overlap between fun and talent and passion and purpose, and even how we carve out a living in the world, for now let's think of fun as its own destination.

On the page at least, I've always understood the importance of fun. In my very first novel, *Ready to Fall*, I gave my heroine Beth a fun and totally made-up job as a quote researcher. (Can I tell you how many women have emailed me over the years to ask where they can find a job like that?) Sarah in *Must Love Dogs* is a preschool teacher. To this day what I miss most about my own teaching days are all the fun things I used to get to do with the kids—scarf juggling, open ocean rowing, multicultural games and dance.

March in *Multiple Choice* goes to college when her daughter does and gets an internship at a radio station. In *Life's a Beach*, Ginger makes sea glass jewelry and her boyfriend Noah is a glass blower. Bella in *Summer Blowout* is a makeup artist. In *The Wildwater Walking Club*, Noreen, Rosie and Tess walk and talk and talk and walk and get their lives back on track. Jill in *Seven Year Switch* works for a company called Great Girlfriend Getaways, and Sandy in *Best Staged Plans* is a home stager. Deirdre in *Wallflower in Bloom* competes on *Dancing with the Stars*, and Melanie in *Time Flies* is a metal sculptor.

Tough work but somebody's gotta do it! Writing these novels gave me a great excuse to learn more about new worlds, to try fun things under the guise of research. I wasn't always conscious of it at the time, but hindsight 20/20, I think I was trying to shovel more of the fun I craved into my own life.

It makes me so happy when readers tell me that a heroine in one of my novels has inspired them to try something fun. But I think it's time to step it up. Because when it comes to fun, there are some awesome possibilities out there for all of us.

Outside In or Inside Out

As someone who has been known to live almost entirely in my head, it seems a bit odd to make our next stop physical awesomeness, but somehow it also feels right. I'm stretched out in a really comfortable chair watching Barbara Walters interview Oprah Winfrey for her *Most Fascinating People of the Year* special, which I recorded ages ago and am finally getting around to watching.

Barbara asks Oprah what horizons are left for her.

The weight, Oprah says. *Always the weight.*

As my own weight has crept up and up along with the years, I've mostly managed not to think about it. When it's momentarily brought to my attention by an evil photo or a disastrous session in a store dressing room, I say things to myself like, *Yeah, big deal—but look at all the books I've written!*

Like the two things are mutually exclusive. You know, as if writing books and looking good are the equivalent of trying to pat your head and rub your stomach at the same time. And if you stretch the comparison a bit, it's even kind of true. As great as the last decade and a half of my life has been, it's also been filled with plenty of stress, and in order to write 14 books during that same span of time, I've spent way, way too much time sitting at my computer.

We all know by now that too much stress and too much sitting can lead to weight gain. But I'm long past my dieting era, yo-yoing up and down and up and down again, only to end up weighing more at the end of each vicious cycle.

Instead, I've managed to come up with a few brilliant solutions of my own. I've stopped weighing myself. I practically live in black yoga pants and baggy T-shirts. When I can't get away with those, I wear long, flowy things that feel vaguely diva-ish and sometimes even come in ego-stroking single-digit sizes like 0, 1, 2, and 3. I've also added an assortment of "travel clothes," not only wrinkle-free but with the added bonus of being seriously stretchy, which I wear even when I'm not actually traveling.

But there's more than ego and vanity hidden beneath my denial. The truth is I'm not feeling all that great. I get my writing done. I travel to my speaking gigs. I walk every day, or at least almost every day. But by the time early evening rolls around, I don't have the energy for much beyond curling up with a book or spacing out in front of some mindless TV.

I try to come up with an image of how I'm feeling. The best I can do is this: It feels like I'm physically blocking my own light.

Barbara and Oprah wrap it up. As I click the remote, I decide a key step on my path to awesomeness will be putting in the time to figure out my own personal solution to the weight thing once and for all.

At this point, I'm not even thinking that I want a body that says awesome in a whole new way. I just want my energy back. I want to feel better.

A Notebook

Our next step is to choose a Shine On notebook. I imagine us all skipping up and down the aisles of a store together, singing *a notebook, a notebook, a green and yellow notebook* at the top of our lungs to the tune of our childhood "A-Tisket, A-Tasket."

But in reality, I only have to roll my chair across a short stretch of hardwood floor and open a closet. While more organized women might have fully stocked gift closets, my home office closet, which started off housing disparate things like a scanner, a mammoth roll of bubble wrap, and a file box jam-packed with publishing contracts, has pretty much morphed into a notebook closet.

If you've read *Never Too Late*, you already know I'm a big fan of notebooks. Whenever I start writing a new book, I break open a fresh one. I have a whole stack of notebooks filled with quotes that have touched or inspired me in some way. I often take notes while I read, writing down lines and passages that are funny or beautifully structured or that I don't want to forget. I've even been known to whip out a small note-book in a dark movie theater to scrawl a particularly brilliant snippet of dialog across a page that I can only hope I haven't already written on since I can't actually see it. I know, a little weird, but I can't help myself.

I know I could type my notes on my phone, but there's just something more satisfying about scrawling the words on paper. And experts say that forming the letters with our hand engages our brains more actively than merely selecting letters to press. Plus, there are so many great notebooks out there.

I have smaller notebooks scattered everywhere so I can jot down ideas wherever they come to me, because otherwise I know I'll forget them five minutes later. I also stockpile notebooks to use for giveaways at book events and reinvention workshops.

This penchant for notebooks has come in handy over the years: When my first book has been published but I'm still teaching at a small private school, instead of having a holiday party one year, all the teachers are transported via fancy bus to a Boston Pops Orchestra holiday performance. I'm searching for a culminating scene for the original *Must Love Dogs* novel, and suddenly I realize I've stumbled upon the perfect location. As the music fills the theater, the whole thing begins to take shape in my head.

I pull a battered notebook from my purse and start writing down all the authentic details—the high cushy seats and multiple hanging TVs on the bus, the ornate theater lobby, the scattering of questionable holiday-themed clothing surrounding me, the arrangement of the musicians on the stage below and the songs they're playing, the chorus of whispers and side comments in our nosebleed high balcony seats.

Even though I'm shielding my notebook and writing as furtively as possible, I can feel a couple of my then teaching colleagues looking over at me with some serious *what is her problem* attitude. But I do it anyway, and it gives me everything I need to finish *Must Love Dogs*. I still have the notebook and the concert program.

If you're not as into notebooks as I am, there are lots of

other good options. You could create a file on your computer. Or a virtual Shine On board (public or private) on Pinterest. Or a collection of Notes on your phone or tablet.

Whatever your choice, you can use it to hold anything and everything you find that will lead you to awesome. I go with a basic college-lined composition notebook covered in a bright retro pattern. And then I can't resist—I cut out the world cloud star I've already printed out and tape it on the cover.

I'm ready to shine.

Negativity: Just Say No

Since I work from home, Facebook is my water cooler. I start paying attention to all the Facebook posts about getting older. The vast majority of them are negative, usually under the guise of trying to be funny.

I'm sure you've seen them, too. The cartoons of aging women with long, saggy breasts. *Growing older is the pits. We're getting to the age where everything falls apart.* That old saw about multi-tasking for seniors means laughing, coughing, sneezing, farting, and peeing all at the same time. The senility prayer. And that *Cat in the Hat* takeoff about aging that has lines like *my memory shrinks/my hearing stinks/* and *no sense of smell/I look like hell.*

I love to laugh. I love to make people laugh. But this kind of thing beats us down, makes us feel less than. And even though it's presented in a joking way, the truth is that it's more mean-spirited than funny.

I don't want to make you feel bad if your Facebook wall is covered in these things. I've probably done it, too, not even thinking as I shared or commented on something, just getting sucked in to the flow. But now that I'm trying to figure out how to grow awesome instead of old, these posts make me cringe. Big time. And worse, they make me feel older.

I think we should all knock it off. Quit feeding into that mentality. Stop tarnishing our image. Rebel against the concept of becoming less with each passing year. Because the more we joke about it, the more we believe it, and the more we believe it, the more we focus on the worst-case getting-older symptoms down the road, many of them completely avoidable, instead of the joy and possibility.

I don't pretend to have it all figured out, but one thing I know so far is that ageist negativity is definitely not the path to awesome. Neither is joining the negativity police. You know, the people who spend all day saying *gotcha* about everyone who breaks the rules—the neighbor who shouldn't be wearing that miniskirt, the guy who didn't wipe down the machines at the gym, the meteorologist who forecasted the weather wrong *again*. You can spend all day pointing out other people's mistakes—and even if you're barely 30 right now, you'll be old before you know it.

Or you can get a life, one that's so interesting you don't have time to notice who's doing what wrong when.

Negativity I write in big letters on the first page of my Shine On notebook. And then I find my favorite turquoise marker, circle the word, and draw a great big diagonal line through it.

Insert Positivity Here

Several years ago: I've been invited to speak at the Savannah Book Festival, and so I also offer to teach a writing workshop for a group of literacy teachers while I'm there. I'm not sure exactly what pieces I have that might be helpful to them, so when the day comes I throw in everything I can think of. Writing activities I've used with adults and kids. The details of a middle school book club I'd once started back in my teaching days.

A quick show of hands lets me know that many of the literacy teachers are also writers, so I share my own writing journey, as well as tips and strategies for writing a book and getting it published. They ask lots of good questions and I do my best to answer them.

After the event, I sign books for everybody. As I finish signing hers, a woman says, "You're the most positive person I've ever met."

I give her a big smile. "What a nice thing to say. Thanks for making my day."

She hands me what appears to be a hair elastic and walks away.

I just figure she thought I'd dropped it, even though I

don't actually have enough hair for a ponytail. I put it down on the table and move on to the next person.

When I finally get to the end of the signing line, I pick up the stretchy little circle with two fingers and take a closer look. Engraved on a tiny metal strip on it is the word *positivity*. I do some Googling when I get back to my hotel room and find out that the bracelets are worn by cancer survivors and their supporters.

Even though I'd written it on her book, I've forgotten the woman's name by now so I can't track her down to thank her again. I have no idea if she's fighting cancer or if someone close to her is. But if she's reading this now, I'd like her to know that bracelet means a lot to me.

I believe that positivity can change our lives. That like attracts like, and optimism opens our hearts and feeds our souls. That anything can happen if we believe it can, as long as we're willing to put in the work.

As I try to figure out how to grow awesome instead of old, I decide to renew my focus on staying positive. I'm going to consciously develop an attitude of

gratitude. I'm going to cultivate positivity until it blooms into a lush garden of optimism, bright and cheery and hopeful.

Positivity, I write in orange marker on a fresh page in my notebook. I circle it and add lines radiating out until it looks vaguely like a sun. Then I doodle flowers all over the page, giving every bright marker I can find a turn.

As a doodler, I'm a total hack. I'm sure there are fourth graders who draw flowers better than I do. Maybe even preschoolers.

I have no doodling aptitude. I'm talentless. I'll never hit a doodling bestseller list. I have zero motivation to try to get better at it, to see where my doodling can take me.

And that's what makes it fun. Doodling makes me feel like a kid again.

Notebook Planning

It probably took me longer than it should have to catch on to the fact that doing a little bit every day works astonishingly better than thinking about something all day long and doing nothing. It took me even longer to figure out that doing a little bit every day works amazingly better than doing a lot one day and then nothing for the next three days, or three months, or three years.

Because if you do that little bit every day, day in and day out, eventually it becomes a lifelong habit. And that's what we're going for.

Embracing this system has given me the gift of my midlife career. I've been writing two polished pages a day seven days a week since 2000. Which is why I'm writing my 15th book now and not still hoping to get around to my first.

So we're going to commit to writing in our Shine On notebook every day. One word. One sentence. One page. One doodle. Whatever. As our notebooks take on a life of their own, the way every book I've ever written eventually has, we'll find our unique paths to shining on.

"Writing is an exploration," E. L. Doctorow said. "You start from nothing and learn as you go."

Clearly I'm a pantser. I like to wing it, to feel my way through, to stay open to the surprises along the way, to let structure emerge organically.

If you're a plotter, a planner, an outliner, a scheduler, then obviously this will never do. So every day you might want to write three things in your notebook:

- One fun thing you did today
- One other step you took toward awesome
- One inspiring quote

I'll go first, just to try it out.

FUN: Today I took a Zumba class, which is basically dance aerobics with a Latin twist, something I've been telling myself I don't have time to do. I was pretty rusty, and I felt like I needed to borrow The Tin Man's oilcan. The good news is I can still do a mean shimmy. I loved the music, loved being unplugged from my computer and phone for an hour, and it made me remember how much I've always loved to dance.

AWESOME STEP: I've zeroed in on the ways I've been eating wrong, hopefully in time to save myself from feeling and looking crappy for the rest of my life, as well as from irreversible brain damage. Oops, so much for positivity!

QUOTE: "Your 40s are good. Your 50s are great. Your 60s are fab. And 70 is f*cking awesome. I'm not quite there yet, but almost."—*Helen Mirren*

Maybe structuring your notebook this way will work for you. Or maybe reading this has already triggered a better idea. Personally, I think the everyday repetition of it would make me feel boxed in, itchy even. Or like I'm not being real—you know, as if I'm writing not for me but to give some nonexistent teacher who's grading me whatever it is I think s/he's looking for. Though returning to this structure every once in a while might be a good way for me to get back on track when I need it.

The important thing to remember is that it's our notebook and we can use it any way we want to.

Bucket Lists and F*ckIt Lists

For a while there, it was all about the Bucket List. You know, all the larger-than-life things we're going to do once before we kick it. Climb Mount Kilimanjaro. Eat centipedes. Run a marathon. Buy an island. Bungee jump.

But for me, a F*ckIt List has turned out to be a far more valuable tool.

You've heard the stories. I've certainly written the novels. About the woman who, after dating a veritable potpourri of wrong men, finally says, *That's it. I give up. F*ckIt.* So she puts her energy into enjoying her solo life. And the very next week she bumps smack into a great guy at a street fair or the gym.

When I walked away from almost 14 years of traditional publishing to publish my books myself, it was one of the biggest F*ckIt moments of my life. But my career had become increasingly soul crushing, so it was time. The scariest part was letting go of the advances (money paid to an author after signing a book contract) that were paying my bills.

But I also had to say F*ckIt to every author's dream: hitting the *New York Times* bestseller list. It's something you might pretend not to care about, but making that list gives you prestige. It's one of the measures, a door opener, something you can claim for the rest of your life.

Just in case you don't already know this, bestseller lists aren't about a book's total sales. They're based on sales during a single week. When publishers really, really want an author's book to hit that list, they manipulate every variable they can to try to make it happen: pushing preorders (preorder sales are added to the first week's sales), rallying the sales team, creating a carefully orchestrated weeklong blitz of media and author events.

My own sales tended to happen over time, as my fabulous readers recommended my books to friends, and word-of-mouth built from there. But the more I learned about the business and my readership increased, the more I believed hitting that list was within the realm of possibility if the publisher would make my next book one of the chosen. I pushed. My publishers made promises but never quite seemed to follow through. The cycle repeated. And repeated. I have to admit I was more than a little bit pissed off.

One of the things I did when I went out on my own was to move hitting the *New York Times* bestseller list from my Bucket List to my F*ckIt List. If it didn't happen when I was with my powerful New York publishers, it certainly wasn't going to happen when Marshbury Beach Books, aka little ol' me, was handling my books solo. So I took a deep breath and let the dream go.

Fast forward less than two years later and I'm running a promotion for one of the 11 books I now own. I've had some pretty good success doing this. In fact, I've hit the *USA Today* bestseller list, another big list, with several different books already this year with the same kind of promotion. And this book makes the *USAT* list, too, but it hits much higher on it than my other ones have.

I can't even let the possibility in on a conscious level, but something makes me casually scroll through the *New York Times* site when the new lists post online the next day. And there it is. I'm a freakin' *New York Times* bestselling author. In a career that might look glamorous from the outside but can make you feel less than as often as not, it's a very big deal.

The timing is freaky. My first book is published on May 1, 2000. I become a *New York Times* bestselling author on May 1, 2015. May Day! May Day!

Hitting that list proves once again that it is never, EVER too late.

Hot tears roll down my face. Even though I know it's an overused image, I can't help but think of Dorothy clicking her shiny red patent leathers together in *The Wizard of Oz* and realizing she has the power all along. I briefly consider running out for a celebratory tattoo, maybe Dorothy's shoes with a banner over them that says *NYT Bestselling Author* in fancy letters. Instead I create my own temporary tattoo by writing *NYT* on the inside of my wrist with a bright purple Sharpie. It's enough.

Even when it doesn't magically trigger a happy ending, a F*ckIt List can come in handy. I've added lots of things to mine to help let them go. My imperfect teeth (when you grow up as one of eight kids, your teeth need to be *really* bad to get braces). All those cleome seeds I planted in my garden that never even sprouted. The stupid thing that popped out of my mouth at a party or during an interview. The fact that a certain person I can't avoid always goes out of her way to let me know she doesn't like me. F*ckIt. F*ckIt all.

So nothing against Bucket Lists, but you might want to consider starting a F*ckIt List in your notebook, too.

A Quick Note on Language

So it seems that I've already dropped a few *f*-bombs. You might be shaking your head at my good girl need to soften them with a carefully placed *. Or you could just as easily be pursing your lips at my completely uncalled for vulgarity.

Personally, I think a little bit of energetic swearing in the right company can be invigorating as well as cathartic. It's a great way to blow off steam to someone you trust when someone else has done you wrong, or the world has demonstrated that it's an even crazier place than you already thought it was.

Betty White is my role model here. She manages to strike the perfect balance between wicked and adorable when she unleashes her inner potty mouth. It's refreshingly outrageous, and she makes me want to grow up to be just like her.

When I was a child, the adults around me never swore, at least not so I noticed. My early elementary school years were spent at parochial school, where the nuns who taught us weren't big swearers either. So the first four-letter words I heard came out of the mouths of my contemporaries. Because of that, I somehow thought the words themselves had been invented by the kids and that adults didn't even know them. True story, I swear.

To this day, those words still retain a little bit of that secret language quality for me. If someone feels comfortable enough around me to loosen up her vocabulary, I take it as a sign that she's let me in.

My old friend Lory (not that we're old!) once gave me a dictionary of the weirdest words in the world. Its pages include a fair share of unusual swear words, from clinchpoop (jerk) to clishmaclaver (foolish gossip) to cockabaloo (bullying boss) to cockalorum (a little man with delusions of grandeur). It's a great resource for a writer, and a fun way to break things up now and then. But as far as off-color language goes, in my opinion there's nothing like one of the old faithfuls.

Even James Lipton, host of the long-running *The Actor's Studio*, who is hardly a laid back kind of guy, encourages his guests to swear. In fact, *What's your favorite curse word?* is the show's most popular question. Some of the actors get pretty creative, but most of them prefer the classic words just like I do. (In case you were wondering, f*ck is the most popular.)

So if swearing in the right company feels good to you, let 'er rip. If you're not sure, try it—you might like it. At the very least you might be able to freak out your adult and semi-adult kids. If it's not your thing, that's okay, too. Just don't waste your time doing the gotcha thing and lecturing the rest of us about our language. You've got way more important things to do with your time. In fact, you might want to go have some fun instead.

Jumping Off the Food Pyramid

Am I the only one who missed the memo? That the food pyramid, which was created in 1992, never really held up, but the U.S. government had already sunk a ton of money into it, so they just let it hang around and continue to misinform us, deluding us into thinking we were making healthy choices for ourselves and our children.

And even though the food pyramid was updated somewhat with MyPlate back in 2010, lots of people think it was too little too late. There's now a huge chasm between the doctors and nutritionists who still buy into the high carb, low fat, calorie-counting, portion control way of eating and those who say grains and sugar are making us fat and sick, and if we simply ditch those, we'll not only lose weight, but our health will improve dramatically.

I'm not a nutritionist or a physician, but I'm a really good reader. So I read all the books I can get my hands on: *Why We Get Fat and What To Do About It, Grain Brain, Wheat Belly Total Health* and lots more.

That's me! I say again and again as I read. I realize that what I've been feeling is my blood sugar bouncing around all over the place. That I'm constantly trying to find the right thing to eat to level it out, to get back to that brief happy place midway between the highest spike and the crash that follows quickly. And the choices I'm making—pasta with veggies and a low-fat sauce, a container of low-fat fruit-flavored yogurt, or a sandwich on whole grain bread—are only making it worse.

Even though I said goodbye to my big hair and leg warmers ages ago, I realize I've stayed stuck in the '80s in terms of nutrition. I'm embarrassed by that. I'm also more than a little bit angry. I feel like I've been duped. Just about the only thing I've been doing right all these years is drinking lots of water.

It's not that I haven't seen the headlines about the damage our diets are doing to us. But I've dismissed them as the latest diet fad, as somebody selling something. You know, one moment eggs are the devil and the next they're a miracle food.

With each book I read, I get a slightly different piece of the puzzle. I decide I've grown increasingly carb sensitive as I've gotten older. So I stop eating all but the healthiest carbohydrates—leafy greens and low carb, cruciferous veggies like broccoli and cauliflower. I ditch grains and sugar and processed foods completely. I add lots of healthy fats—avocados, coconut and olive oil, wild salmon, nuts. When in doubt I eat eggs or a handful of almonds or a hunk of Havarti. Or I defrost some cooked shrimp or open a can of yellow fin tuna packed in olive oil and use it as a salad topper.

And then I wait to see what will happen.

By way of disclaimer, please don't try this at home just because I did. You may be way ahead of me on this food journey, but if you haven't started it yet, do your own reading, your own research. Listen to your own body. Figure out what you believe. Find a way to feel better.

Sitting and Sitting

As I start to write this section, in my head Otis Redding is serenading me with "Sitting on the Dock of the Bay." There's nothing like an occasional lazy day watching the tide roll away, but sitting all day every day is definitely not going to help us shine on. The people who measure these things say we're probably spending somewhere around 70% of our time sitting—in cars, eating, watching TV, working at a computer, reading.

We all probably know by now that too much sitting not only ages us but slowly kills us, increasing our risk for heart disease, diabetes, and obesity along the way. It doesn't seem fair that this is true whether we exercise regularly or not, but fair or unfair, the facts are in.

One study even compares sitting all day to smoking a pack and a half of cigarettes. In one of the many mistakes I've made in my life, as a young teenager I took up smoking to look cool. I quickly progressed from dizzy to addicted and continued to smoke until right before my husband Jake and I decided we were ready to have kids. Quitting smoking was one of the toughest things I've ever done, but I'm proud to say I did it. That the effects of sitting, which is the way I spend most of my day as a writer, are being compared to this nasty, health-destroying habit I left in the dust decades ago is a total bummer.

In the quest to grow awesome instead of old, I know too much sitting is one more thing I definitely need to deal with, and the sooner the better.

I walk just about every day, but what I've been doing is using that walk as a reward for finishing my daily pages. In terms of getting a book written, it works great. I wake up around 5:30 in the morning and sit right down and get to work. By the time I've finished writing, walking looks really good, and I can't wait to lace up my sneakers and hit the road.

But the reality is that by this point I've been sitting and sitting for anywhere from five to eight hours, with occasional breaks to grab something to eat or go to the bathroom. After I walk, I sit down again to answer email and interview questions, to check in on Facebook and Twitter. And then I sit down some more to eat, to read, to watch a movie.

Not good. (And Roberta Flack is singing "Killing Me Softly" now.)

I know a few women who work at treadmill desks, but I can't even read while walking on a treadmill (or sitting in a moving car) without getting really nauseated, so I know this isn't the way to go for me.

A standing desk is another option. But I've learned the hard way over the years not to just run out and buy a big ticket item like this, because if it doesn't work out it'll just turn into an overpriced cat perch. So as a first step, I Google up makeshift versions of standing desks. I find a link to a cool one made out of stacks of soda cans. Maybe I could give the one I make a healthier vibe by using seltzer cans instead.

I flash back to college and the coffee tables a bunch of the kids on my dorm floor are assigned to make out of soda cans for a class they're taking. Some of them are really creative—Christmas tree lights weaving in and out of the cans or a philodendron growing from a soil-filled pot hidden in the center under a Plexiglas top.

And then one day someone drops a heavy backpack on one, or several people plop down all at once on another during a keg party. Eventually, all the soda can coffee tables come tumbling down. My office isn't quite as wild as a college dormitory, but my cats have been known to whoop it up a bit, and I'd like to save my precious iMac from a similar fate.

I find another makeshift standing desk online that's been made for $22 from Ikea parts and even has step-by-step directions. I'm about to jump in the car to make an Ikea run when I remember that, for me, shopping of any kind is almost always a stall tactic.

I look around my office for inspiration. I've certainly got plenty of books, so I just grab a bunch of big ones and pile them under my iMac until it's standing height. Then I arrange my keyboard and mouse on top of a shorter stack of books.

It works pretty well, in a rickety kind of way. A quick trial makes me realize I can't actually think of anything to write while I'm standing, although that will probably come in time.

Then it occurs to me that while standing is definitely better than sitting, it's not moving, which is what I really need to do. Worse, now I'm afraid to walk away from my desk in case my iMac starts to topple over while I'm gone.

I decide to revisit the standing desk thing later. I pull the books out from under my computer and keyboard, put them back on my bookshelf.

Then I sit down so I can think.

Wherever We Go, There We Are

I lived for many years in Scituate, Massachusetts, a terrific beach town halfway between Boston and Cape Cod. I write beachy books. One is even called *Life's a Beach*. And if you'd asked me where Jake and I would end up once we were ready to downsize as empty nesters, I would have told you, with complete confidence, another beach town.

As Jacques Cousteau said, "The sea, once it casts its spell, holds one in its net of wonder forever."

The beach is my happy place. I don't like lounging around in the hot sun. I rarely venture into the ocean above my knees, perhaps the result of watching *Jaws* for the first time during my highly suggestible teen years. But to walk the beach, especially as the sun rises or sets, is pure heaven to me. The feel of the sand between my toes. The smell of the salt air. The rhythm of the waves. The swooping of the gulls. It's soothing. It's epic. Time and time again, the sea brings me back to me.

After way too many cold New England winters spent working outdoors as a land surveyor, the one thing Jake really, really wanted was to say goodbye to cold and snow. So we spent years looking for a more temperate sea, a warmer version of our cool beach town. We surfed the Internet, swam through oceans of virtual tours, built lists of likely prospects like sandcastles. We spent our vacations visiting as many of these beach towns as we could and ruling them in or out as possibilities.

And then we moved to Metro Atlanta.

In a curriculum call I will never understand, when I was in junior high back before it was renamed middle school, the honors kids at my school got to skip U.S. Geography and take another year of World History instead. As a result, I still remember that England was the first country to industrialize, and I could maybe even tell you a little bit about the Mayan Empire or the Russian Revolution or the Tang Dynasty. But my geography skills are so pathetic that I'm not sure I could reliably name all 50 states, let alone find them on a map if you hid the names on me.

But even I know that Atlanta isn't anywhere near an ocean.

Our two adult kids both ended up living there though. So after all those years of beach town hunting, when push came to shove, it turned out that for us family trumped everything, including proximity to a beach.

There are people who will advise you never to move to be near your grown children. Because what if you uproot your whole life and leave everything you know, and then your kids pack up and move again? Or what if your kids don't move, but instead you end up spending all your time helping them out instead of building a new life of your own? *Don't make yourselves too accessible*, these people say. *Keep a healthy distance.*

Whenever I find myself in a beach town like the one I might have moved to, I make it a point to connect with midlife women—at the visitors center or walking the beach—so I can ask them if they live around here. If it turns out they do, I ask how long they've been here and where they came from and if it's been a good move for them.

Some are incredibly happy to be living their beach dream.

But a surprising number of the women I've chatted with feel isolated. *I miss my son*, one woman said to me recently. *We're really close and I don't think I appreciated that enough when I lived near him. I'd move back in a heartbeat if I could put all the pieces together.*

Oh, I miss my grandchildren terribly, another woman said. *Playing with them when they visit makes me feel alive again.*

We're all different, so only you can figure out this part of the journey for yourself. But for Jake and me, the decision to pack up and follow our kids to Atlanta has worked out really well. Holidays are easy breezy now. All the stress—who's flying in when, how late their flight will be, how bad the traffic is—is gone. There's no more pressure to try to turn a visit into something worthy of a Norman Rockwell painting or at least a Hallmark card. Because in the very best way, a holiday is just another day now.

We're all really busy so it's not like we hang out in one another's back pockets. But we're right there whenever anybody needs something. It's so convenient to be able to watch one another's dogs and cats, especially since we have eight of them between us. And those impromptu cookouts and spur of the moment shopping trips are worth more to me than all the sand on any beach.

Like the rest of life, it's not perfect. North Georgia is lush and beautiful, and the people here are super friendly. But the traffic in this neck of the woods is a nightmare, and the massive highways terrify me. The area we live in is big and sprawling, a city masquerading as a suburb. A charming little beach town it's not.

Still, I'm happy here, at least for this chapter of my life. The move has pushed me out of my comfort zone, helped me grow both as a writer and as a person. Change is good.

But what I'm realizing as I set my sights on awesome is that I've fallen into the trap of postponing fun. Waiting until I can click out of work mode long enough to spend a few days at the beach, which is now a 5½ hour drive or a plane ride away instead of two minutes down the road. I'm definitely not taking advantage of the fun that's right in my backyard. In fact, even though I've been here for a few years now, I'm not even sure what *is* in this new backyard.

It's so easy to put our lives on hold until this, that, or the other thing happens. I need to work on that. I mean, play with that.

Food Transition

Jimmy Buffet is singing "Cheeseburger in Paradise." He's really getting on my nerves, possibly because I know *his* cheeseburger is sandwiched in a fat white bun, while mine is wrapped up in two flimsy romaine leaves. And he's probably got a margarita going too, while I'm abstaining from alcohol until I get this low carb thing down.

I take another long slug of water. I'm surprised at how crappy I feel. It's as if I'm almost, but not quite, coming down with the flu. Or like I'm detoxing, which I guess I am. My head aches. I have even less energy than I did when I started eating this way. I'm not really hungry, or maybe it's more that I'm not all that interested in food now that starch and sugar are off the table.

I Google up carbohydrate withdrawal and there I am. All my symptoms are apparently the result of the transition from a high carb to a low carb, grain-and sugar-free diet. I keep reading. We ditched our saltshaker years ago, but I follow the advice I find and start salting my food again (and discover pink Himalayan rock salt) and taking magnesium citrate (the citrate part is important) to ward off constipation, another side effect of this transition phase.

I decide I'll give it some time. I'll just hang around and not expect too much of myself for a while beyond writing my daily pages and having a little bit of fun. If I don't feel better after two weeks, maybe I'll stop at the grocery store and pick up a deep-dish pizza.

I might even eat the whole thing.

Bouncing Back

I eat a handful of almonds and wander around my house while I drink my coffee. Since I have about as much oomph as a slug right now, I've got my hopes for the day pinned on multitasking. I'm looking for something that will help me meet my daily page quota, have some fun, and take one more step toward awesome all at the same time.

I notice an exercise ball tucked into a corner of a bedroom that's a completely inefficient cross between a nonfunctional exercise room, a bed-less guest room, a book depository, and an overflow closet. It's a nice shade of purple even from a distance.

I've never actually used this exercise ball. It was given to me by someone who was moving and had never used it either. It had been given to her by someone else who never used it. It's pristine, virginal even. I keep thinking I'll find the right person to give it to, so she can never use it, too. Or that one of our cats will decide to play with it one day and claw a hole in it. Then I can throw it away without feeling guilty.

I roll it into my office, move my desk chair out of the way. The moment I sit down on this exercise ball, I love it. I can type, no problem. Bouncing a little even helps me think. I feel my abdominal and back muscles working as I make tiny circles, first clockwise and then counterclockwise. I lift my right foot off the ground and extend my leg to make sitting on it more challenging. I take it up a notch and extend my left hand over my head at the same time. Then I switch arms and legs.

I know I'm still sitting, but it feels like a much more active kind of sitting. I realize I'm also sitting up straighter, simply because the exercise ball makes me do this so I don't fall off.

It's awesome. It's fun. I get my daily pages written. Even the bright purple exercise ball seems happy to be finally getting a workout.

Your Version of My Pages

So, we're writing in our Shine On notebooks every day. I'm also writing my two pages a day, seven days a week. Finishing those pages each day is the thing that moves me forward in my life, the biggest ticket item in my quest for enduring awesomeness. If I stopped writing them, my whole house of cards would eventually collapse.

Writing those daily pages is also my North Star. Whenever I start to get lost, whenever I'm overwhelmed by too many choices or the urge to procrastinate, those pages pull me back on track.

Trying to do something that's important to you as well and as consistently as you can is not at all the same as trying to do everything perfectly. In a way it's the opposite. You pick the big thing and cut yourself some slack on everything else.

Clarity is important here. If you haven't chosen a goal, you can't get there. Being able to identify your most important task, to make it a priority and do it to the very best of your ability until you finish it, day in and day out, is a very big deal. It's also really hard. Most people don't do it. They get distracted. Or discouraged. But if I had to pick one path that will help lead us to our own unique versions of shining on, this is it.

So I'm suggesting that you pick the single biggest, hardest, most important thing you can think of so far, besides writing in your notebook every day, that will lead you to awesome. Do it first every day. In the beginning it will take motivation and willpower, but eventually it will become habit, which will make it a teensy bit easier. And the bright side is that if you do the tough thing first, everything you do for the rest of your day will feel easier by comparison. As opposed to doing the hardest thing last and letting it hang over your head all day.

You might not have a big-ticket item that feels to you the way my writing feels to me, at least not yet. That's okay.

I'm not much of a list maker, but even I think it might be a good idea to make one at this point. So let's list the five things we know so far that will help lead us to awesome. Some of these are going to change as we move along, but let's just do the best we can for now. Arrange them in order, the most important one first.

If you're reading the ebook version of this book, you can write your list using the Notes feature. If you're reading a paper book, grab the nearest pen. Either way, copy your list over in your Shine On notebook. Dog ear the page or flag it with a Post-It.

Okay, I'll go first.

Shine On List: Mine

1. Write my daily pages.
2. Have some fun.
3. Reinvent the way I eat.
4. Move more.
5. Try new things and find out which ones work for me.

Shine On List: Yours

1.
2.
3.
4.
5.

For now at least, #1 is your big-ticket item. It should be a stretch. It might even scare you a bit. But you're pretty sure that if you stay on task, it will help lead you to the awesome version of you.

Figure out a way to break down your big-ticket item into a daily plan like my two pages a day. Maybe you'll spend fifteen minutes or an hour a day on it. Or you'll take one step a day in that direction. Whatever makes sense.

But you're absolutely going to do it every day. And if you don't get to the rest of your list, that's okay.

#1 is the one you're going to fight. You'll want to save it for later, even though we're all old enough to know by now how often life gets in the way and later never happens. Don't let yourself get lost in all the minutia of your life. Don't tell yourself you're going to work your way up to #1 by doing the smaller, easier things first.

The amount of time it takes to finish your big-ticket item, the one that will really help you shine on, is often the exact same amount of time it takes to do something that isn't all that necessary in the scheme of things, like vacuuming. So do it first every day if you can, even if it means getting up early or juggling something else. The difference can be life changing.

And remember, nothing happens unless you make it happen.

Origami Fail

So my purple exercise ball and I have finished writing my daily pages, and now I'm looking for a little fun. On one of my bookshelves I discover a six-inch square box containing an origami calendar—essentially a year's worth of origami paper and folding instructions, each one with a date on it.

It's never been opened. I can no longer remember if someone gave it to me as a gift, or if someone gave it to one of my kids and I inherited it when they rejected it. Who knows, maybe it was given to me by the same person who gave me the purple exercise ball.

In any case, I know how old it is because it's a 2005 calendar. And in all that time I've neither used it a single time nor thrown it away. I think I held onto it because it looked like it might be fun, but once again I've postponed fun, this time for an entire decade.

I break open the box and pull out a page of general instructions, symbols, and techniques. I hate instructions, or *intrucksions* as Riley, Ginger's nephew in *Life's a Beach*, calls them. I force myself to focus. An arrow pointing down means push, and an arrow pointing up means pull. A circle with a curved arrow at the end means flip over. A cloud with an arrow on one side means blow in here.

You blow in there, I say out loud to no one in particular.

There's an inside reverse fold and an outside reverse fold, a mountain fold and a valley fold, a squash technique and a sink technique. I can feel an origami headache coming on. I take a deep breath and try to hang in there.

Even though I've been ignoring this little box forever, I want to love origami so much. I love the shiny squares of brightly colored paper. I love the elaborate surprise, the way a bunch of folds can somehow come together to create a miniature masterpiece. I want to work my way up to the March canoe, move on to the September panda, to the pink November pig.

I mess up immediately by not even choosing the right piece of origami paper. Somehow I miss the page that says: *Don't throw this page away. Use it to fold the nightingale.* I select the nightingale directions page instead, which means I can't read them once I start folding. Though in my defense they shouldn't have printed the directions on origami paper if they didn't want me to do this.

So apparently the way it works is that you follow the directions on one page while folding another, and then the next day you fold that page while you read the directions on the next page. I'm thoroughly confused by this notion and also really glad that I write books and not origami calendars. But I decide I'm going to stay with it long enough to at least make the January 1st nightingale. I mean, I can only imagine the calendar creator will assume that everyone has been out partying the night before and go easy on us.

Belatedly, I select the correct square of origami paper and begin. The first steps to make the nightingale are not so bad, but somewhere between the valley fold, rotating the model, and folding the front flap up, I get totally lost. The two dimensional pictures just don't seem to translate to the three dimensional folds I'm trying to make. This should be easy, but it's really, really hard for me. It not only makes me feel like a total loser, but also makes me want to quit mid-nightingale.

As part of my research for this book, I've been reading about our brains and how to keep them sharp as we age, since it's hard to imagine shining on without a brain that's firing on all cylinders.

I've learned that it's important to engage in new and complex activities, things that are difficult for us, things that initially make us frustrated or feel like quitting. Because when we hang in, our brains will develop more neurons to make the activity easier. We're actually forcing our brains to keep growing.

Well, let me tell you, I'm creating so many new neurons right now that fireworks are going off in my head and smoke might even be coming out of my ears. I finally finish my nightingale and give its wings a little flap. It doesn't look like even a distant cousin to the picture in the instructions. Instead of a cute little pointy beak, my nightingale has an extra long nose that reminds me of Pinocchio's.

I tape my pathetic nightingale on a page of my notebook to remind me that I don't have to be perfect. I tell myself that the good news is I'm feeling smarter already.

I have to admit I still hate origami though. But maybe you won't. And if so, would you please make me a panda bear?

Getting Better All the Ti-i-ime

Even if The Beatles weren't singing "Getting Better" to me, I'd be feeling so much better. My flulike symptoms and sluggishness have completely disappeared. Suddenly my energy is back, my head is clear, my cravings are gone, my blood sugar has stopped bouncing around all over the place. My daily pages are practically writing themselves. Okay, that last one's a lie, but I can dream.

I'm eating clean and simply. Healthy fats, lot of greens and fresh low-carb veggies, eggs high in omega 3s, wild salmon, nuts and seeds, avocado, grass fed beef, a little bit of cheese, no grains, no sugar. I simply cannot believe how much better I feel eating like this.

It's easy, too. I can pretty much eat whatever everyone around me is eating. I just ditch the bread or the pasta and turn it into a salad. I've always loved salads, but making one often felt like too much work, so I'd grab something quicker. But now when I'm faced with the choice of a salad or nothing, I'm motivated to wash that lettuce, and it's really not such a big deal after all.

I'm so surprised that I don't feel the least bit deprived, though I'm definitely a lot less interested in food now. I eat when I'm hungry—what a concept! I stop eating when I'm not hungry. The food I'm eating doesn't make me hungry again an hour and a half or two hours later. If I were a foodie, I'd probably have to find another hobby, but for me it's kind of a relief to move thinking about food to the back burner. There are so many other things I'd rather think about.

As is often the case when we start to make positive changes in our lives, the sabotage brigade comes out of the woodwork. *How long do you have to keep eating like that?* somebody asks me as she shakes her head sadly. *It's so restrictive.*

Life is short, somebody else says. *Just have a bite or two.*

My truth is that life is too short to keep feeling the way I'd been feeling. My denial has lifted, and I'm able to see that I was probably making my own life even shorter by the way I was eating. I'm proud of myself for making it past that initial tough transition, and I have no urge to go back to the way I used to eat.

I've also read enough to know that this low carb thing is not something you can do a little bit. Even a few bites of the wrong foods might spike my blood sugar levels. The vicious cycle would begin and before I'd know it, I'd be back to square one again. So I just ignore the naysayers.

Judging by the way my clothes fit, or don't fit, weight is melting off my body at a surprisingly fast rate, but I pretty much ignore that, too. I don't want to think of this as a diet. I want it to be about health, not about weight. In fact, I didn't even weigh myself before I started, so I have absolutely no idea how much weight I've lost.

I'm not finding it any more expensive to eat like this, since I'm ignoring most of the square footage of the grocery store. I'm also trying not to obsess. I'm eating so many greens that I try to buy organic whenever I can, but if the organic lettuce looks iffy or wilty or is crazy expensive, I grab the non-organic. Since fat is no longer the enemy, I go for the cheaper, fattier cuts of meat and poultry. And then I feel vaguely guilty and buy grass fed the next time. (So much for not obsessing.)

I've pretty much memorized EWG's (Environmental Working Group) Dirty Dozen yearly list of fruits and vegetable containing high levels of pesticides—apples, celery, cherry tomatoes, cucumbers, grapes, nectarines, peaches, potatoes, snap peas, spinach, sweet bell peppers. I'm not eating some of those things anyway, but I look for organic versions of the ones I do eat. I've got EWG's Clean Fifteen list down, too—asparagus, avocados, cabbage, cantaloupe, cauliflower, eggplant, grapefruit, kiwi, mangoes, onions, papayas, pineapples, corn, sweet peas, sweet potatoes—so as far as the foods I'm eating on that list go, I just grab whatever looks good or is on sale.

Of course, it's not all smooth sailing. Bacon (bacon!) is turning into a dilemma. It's high up on my list of cool things I get to eat in moderation now, and I've managed to find a no-sugar-added brand. And then the World Health Organization comes out with a statement that processed meats cause cancer.

Great, I'm finally feeling better and now I'm going to die a slow, painful bacon death.

Before I do anything drastic like stop eating bacon, I read some more. Yet another expert says that when you cook bacon, any sugars in it are cooked off, just like the alcohol gets cooked off when you cook with wine. So maybe I could buy uncured bacon and cook it long enough to get rid of the sugar, but not so long that the bacon gets crispy, because burned or charred meat is also supposed to be a carcinogen.

Why is life so complicated? Why can't everything in the world be labeled as either good for you or not good for you? I guess it's not quite as bad as origami, but it's still ridiculously confusing.

I decide to make my best guess and go with the uncured sodium nitrite-free bacon. Then I let it go and grab a handful of almonds.

Nature Break

I know I've got to do some moving earlier in the day. But I've spent so many years saving my exercise as a reward for finishing my daily pages that I have to admit I'm a tiny bit superstitious about changing things up. What if I unchain myself from my computer long enough to take a walk before my daily pages are finished, and then I can't get back into my writing when I return?

I can see it already. First I'll miss one day's writing quota and then the next. The downward slide will continue. This book will never materialize. I won't be able to pay my bills. Eventually I'll lose everything—my house, my car, my ability to buy bacon. I'll end up in a doublewide trailer somewhere. And then one day I won't be able to afford even that anymore. I'll have to downsize to a singlewide.

"Whether you think you can or you can't, you're right," Henry Ford said. Or at least people think he's the one who said it. Whatever the source, it's a great way to look at things. Of course I can do this.

The next morning I sit down at my computer at 5:30 and get right to work. Just before 7:30, a shiny green hummingbird hovers outside my office window, peering in at me. This has never happened before, and it feels as if nature has sent a little green messenger, who oddly enough has the exact same beak I gave my origami nightingale, to be my alarm clock. I watch, mesmerized, until it darts off to grab some breakfast in my perennial garden.

I stop writing mid-sentence so I'll have a place to pick up when I get back from my walk. I say goodbye to my purple exercise ball, lace up my sneakers, hit the streets of my neighborhood.

I swing my arms and pick up my pace as Carole King serenades me with "(You Make Me Feel Like) A Natural Woman." It's still cool out, especially by Atlanta's steamy standards. Pink and white and burgundy crepe myrtles are in full bloom. Tall green trees arch over the quiet street.

The moon is fading away in one corner of the cloudless blue sky as the sun pushes its way up in another. A house wren zips through some lower branches—its feisty, vivacious voice makes it a great backup singer for Carole.

Aristotle said, "In all things of nature there is something of the marvelous."

"Look deep into nature, and then you will understand everything better," Albert Einstein said.

Three houses in my little corner of this huge subdivision are being torn down to make way for McMansions. An early crew shows up at one of them and breaks the silence by firing up a backhoe. Joni Mitchell starts singing that line from "Big Yellow Taxi" about paving paradise and putting up a parking lot.

I remember another line from that song, that one about how we don't know what we've got until it's gone. So true. Our health. Our dreams. As I walk by the backhoe, trees tumble over, one by one.

Encroaching McMansions aside, time spent in nature always makes me feel better. I've done enough reading to know that it reduces our stress level, improves our mood, alleviates our anxiety. And even though I'm taking this walk to get more movement into my life, experts say a healthy dose of nature can boost our creativity, too.

I'm hoping those experts are right. I try to keep a part of my head in my book so I'll be able to pick up where I left off.

Not much more than a half hour after I began, I'm back at my desk, reunited with my purple exercise ball. I don't even stop to take my sneakers off because I'm afraid if I start to procrastinate, I'll never get my pages done.

But I get them written in record time. Maybe the walk helped. Maybe it didn't. Maybe it did today, but it won't tomorrow. In any case, I've made the decision to believe I can change things up and still get my writing done.

I feel good. As Georgia O'Keeffe said, "The days you work are the best days."

What Can't Coconut Oil Do?

I discover organic, cold-pressed, unrefined virgin coconut oil. It works well in salad dressings and also stands up to high cooking temperatures. Along with extra-virgin olive oil, I'm using it to replace hydrogenated oils.

I read somewhere that coconut oil is a fabulous moisturizer, too, and when I try it, this turns out to be true for me. My skin drinks it in. I find out it also works great for taking off makeup. When I rub a tiny bit between my hands and run my palms over my hair, it adds shine and helps with the flyaways.

As if that's not enough for something that costs $5.99 a jar at my local Trader Joe's, studies have shown that ingesting coconut oil has many medicinal benefits, from killing bacteria, to increasing our energy expenditure, to making us feel full, to helping with blood sugar and mood. It may even boost brain function.

I'm in. I find out some people stir a tablespoon of coconut oil into their coffee and others lap it right from a spoon. Neither of these options sounds all that appealing to me, so I settle for stirring a tablespoon of it into a glass of warm water in the morning and drinking it down.

Not exactly delicious, but not awful either.

I decide to try to ramp it up to the fun level. Coconut reminds me of Halloween and the long ago days when my friends and I used to turn trick or treating into a marathon. We'd hit neighborhood after neighborhood, filling our pillowcases to the top with candy. We'd go home long enough to drop them off, grab another pillowcase, head off again.

I used to save my Mounds and Almond Joy candy bars to eat last (postponing fun again!) because they were my favorites. Years later they were my first pick when I raided my kids' trick or treat bags.

I wonder if I can come up with a healthy hybrid of the two candy bars—maybe the dark Mounds chocolate mixed with an Almond Joy almond.

I start Googling and there are tons of recipes out there. Apparently there's a whole category of desserts called fat bombs or fat blasters that are supposed to fill you up and keep you happy when you're eating low carb—who knew.

Despite my last name, or maybe because of it, I don't like to cook anymore. I'm with Sandy, my *Best Staged Plans* heroine, when it comes to leaving the cooking phase of her life for the faux cooking phase, which is more about assembling healthy meals from things that other people have at least partially prepared for you.

Since there's no baking involved, I tell myself this isn't really cooking—it's more of a craft project with food. I dust off my old mini muffin pans and find some cute little mini-muffin liners in the back of a cabinet.

I experiment with three different online recipes, combining and tweaking them to simplify as much as I can. Eventually I come up with a treat that tastes like a dark chocolate Mounds Bar with an almond in it. At least if, like me, you haven't had a real Mounds Bar in decades. And you've been away from sugar long enough to have lost your sweet tooth.

If my low-carb journey is not your thing, you can make

these with a regular chocolate bar and sugar. Or just go buy yourself a Mounds Bar or an Almond Joy. Or maybe both.

Midlife Rocks Bars

1 3-oz. Lily's extra dark, stevia sweetened, no added sugar chocolate bar (or 2 bars if you love chocolate!)
24 dry-roasted almonds
½ cup coconut oil
½ cup coconut butter
½ cup unsweetened shredded coconut
2 tablespoons Swerve or powdered stevia (or more or less to taste)

1. Line 24 mini muffin pans with paper liners.
2. Combine coconut oil and coconut butter in a small saucepan. Stir until melted.
3. Remove from heat and add shredded coconut. Stir until mixed. Stir in sweetener, tasting as you go.
4. Spoon equal amounts into muffin pans and freeze.
5. Break or cut candy bar into squares so it will melt more evenly. Place in microwave-safe bowl.
6. Microwave chocolate over low heat for 30 seconds. Stir with spoon or spatula. Keep microwaving at 10-second intervals and stirring so you don't burn it (lesson learned!) until fully melted.
7. Spoon equal portions of melted chocolate over coconut layer.
8. Place an almond on top of each one.
9. Store in freezer. Take one out and thaw at room temperature whenever you need a treat. Or let it thaw in your mouth if you can't wait!

Repairing Old Alliances

I finish my daily pages and check Facebook. The first thing I see in my feed, from a Facebook friend I've never met in the flesh, is this: *Does anyone know who repairs old alliances around here?*

It takes me a moment to realize that her post has been the victim of autocorrect. What she really means to say is *appliances*, not *alliances*.

But even if it's unintentional on her part, this strikes me as a seriously brilliant question.

So who does repair old alliances around here anyway?

We do. In this day and age, if we want to get together with someone, in person or virtually, whether to repair an old friendship, feed a new one, or just to reconnect and have some fun, it's not that hard. We can probably find a way.

I mean to do this a lot. I really do. Then I put it off until after I finish this or do that. And this or that morphs into the next this or that.

As Buddha said, "The trouble is you think you have time."

I ponder this for a while and realize there's another component. Many of these old alliances in my life, and even some of the newer ones, exist in a kind of limbo. There's a lot of *we need to get together* stuff going on. But after months and months, or even years and years of this, it's starting to look like getting together is probably not going to happen. But we're not *not* getting together either—we haven't let it go.

The words start to feel empty after a while. The whole back and forth gets tedious, like an extra weight we're carrying around when we don't have to. It's not a particularly fun or productive way for any of us to spend our time.

Fish or cut bait, my Southern friends might say. My Northern friends would probably change it to *sh*t or get off the pot.*

So in my notebook I make a list of alliances I'd like to repair or reboot or rekindle. I've got some speaking gigs coming up that will take me within striking distance of a couple of these friends. I have some rendezvous ideas for a few others, near and far. I send out emails with specific dates and invitations.

Then I wait to see what will happen.

I hear back from the busiest alliance of the bunch right away. She's in. She's already juggled her schedule to make it work. She has no problem driving to me while I'm speaking not too far from where she lives. We get a plan. We synchronize our schedules. We're good to go.

Another friend emails back with a counter-suggestion. It's a much better idea than the one I'd suggested. We lock it in.

I make plans with another friend for a catch-up phone call.

Somebody else is too busy to schedule anything right now, but she wants to get back in touch with me when things aren't so busy so we can plan something then. Because all she's committing to now are things like x, y, and z, she says, all of which involve getting together with other people. I realize she's B-listing me, maybe even C-listing me. *But we really need to get together*, she finishes. There's my answer.

Yet another alliance goes into full tap dance mode. How much she loves the idea of getting together, the details of why she can't do it and why it's taken her so long to get back to me, how wonderful it is to hear from me, how great it would be to see me. I read it through twice. It's as concrete as air.

Eventually I hear back from everyone. It's split right down the middle: I've got plans with exactly half of them and *we really need to get togethers* from the other half.

I'm surprised that my feelings aren't hurt by my commitment-resistant alliances. Instead I'm relieved to know one way or the other whether they're in or they're out, and my new interpretation of we really need to get together is that they're out. It's freeing not to have to carry these almost plans around any more.

There's no drama. No hard feelings. I still think of all these alliances as friends. I'll still like their posts on Facebook. But I won't play the vague promises game anymore. There's nothing awesome about it.

Fighting Our Inner Dinosaur

Our world is changing at whirlwind speed. And not to bum you out or anything, but right at this very moment, the velocity of the change around us is the slowest it will be for the rest of our lives. The people who know about these things say the changes are just going to keep coming faster and faster and faster.

What this means for all of us is that if we start to resist change, if we hunker down and bury our heads in the sand and hope it will blow right by us, we'll become dinosaurs before we know it.

Because the book world is my lens, one of the examples of this kind of resistance I see all the time has to do with ebooks. Midlife women are often voracious readers, and as a group we've been the biggest early adapters of ebooks.

I mean, what's not to like? Ebooks are often (and should always be) cheaper than paper books, since they cost far less to produce. They don't take up any space on our bookshelves, which are probably already bursting at the seams by this point in our lives. And most of us are also past the accumulating stage and trying to pare down.

Since you can adjust the size of the virtual print, ebooks

are easy on the eyes, and ereaders are often backlit, which makes them even easier on the eyes. But you don't need to buy an ereader to read ebooks. You can download a free app and read them on your tablet, your phone, your computer, all also backlit. There are lots of deals out there, too, so ebooks can be a low-risk way to check out a new author.

Ebooks are immediate gratification in the best sense. If we embrace them, we'll never run out of reading material late at night again, since we can download a new book 24/7 wherever we are. I get emails like this one all the time: *I finished reading Seven Year Switch last night and I didn't know which book of yours to read next. So I downloaded them all. (Might have been that second glass of wine!)*

Which makes me think maybe I should include a bottle of wine with my books. But back to the point, even though many midlife women are huge ebook readers, there are still lots of holdouts. This is what I hear them say: *I want to hold a real book in my hands. I love the smell of paper books. I don't do ebooks.*

I love the smell of paper books, too, as well as the cozy feel of curling up with one in my hands. I still read them, still collect my favorite books in print, autographed by the author if possible. But that doesn't mean I don't also read ebooks. To me that's like saying I won't wire my house for electricity because I like candlelight better. Surely there's room for both in our lives.

Ebooks aren't a religious or a political choice. They're not intrinsically good or bad. But they're here to stay. So why not take advantage of them?

I think what holds us back is the learning curve. With every new thing, there is always a learning curve. Because of that, often we will really, really hate this new thing before we learn to love it.

Before we can read an ebook, we have to find and download the free ebook app to our computer or tablet or phone, or figure out which ereader to buy. Then we have to figure out how to turn on the app or the ereader. How to download the actual ebooks, how to find the little thingamabobbie that makes the font bigger or turns up the backlighting or lets us bookmark passages we like. We have to figure out what to do when we accidentally hit some random button and the whole book disappears.

It's intimidating. It's frustrating. It can make us feel like we're dinosaurs already. But the truth is that when we stop making excuses and push ourselves through the inevitable transition phase, conquering new things is actually what keeps us from *becoming* dinosaurs. So give it a month of actively reading them before you decide whether or not you hate ebooks.

My trick for conquering new things is that I'm convinced there is a free YouTube video to teach us anything in the world we might want to learn, or get us unstuck from wherever it is we just got stuck. So Google one up. Watch the first single step, then pause the video while you do it. Watch the next step. Pause. Do it. Repeat until you're on your way. You don't need to understand it conceptually. You just have to stop overthinking this new thing and follow the steps.

And don't forget, the whole time we're struggling to learn something new, we're forcing our brains to grow, to make new connections. Which means we're absolutely growing awesome instead of old.

These Eyes

It turns out Metro Atlanta has tons of gorgeous parks I haven't yet discovered. I'm looping around one maybe fifteen or twenty minutes from my house. I love to people watch, so I'm checking out everyone I pass and imagining their stories.

I decide the teenagers hanging brightly colored nesting hammocks and slackline tightropes between trees are getting ready to film a pilot for a television show they're planning to pitch to a startup studio. The woman playing the guitar on the bench I just passed is an international spy. The boomer couple holding hands in front of me were high school sweethearts who just found each other again online after all these years. Even the his-and-her dogs they're walking can feel the connection already.

I listen to a symphony of languages and accents as I walk, mining for nuggets of dialog I might be able to use, a tiny notebook and pen tucked into the waistband of my yoga pants just in case. I stop to scratch a sweet mixed breed dog under its graying muzzle and take a moment to miss my own dearly departed Daisy, the shar pei/Lab cross we adopted from a shelter who lived for 15 fabulous years.

When the woman and her dog walk away, I realize I'm

standing in front of a large bulletin board. It's held up by two posts dug into Georgia's famous red clay soil at the edge of the crushed-gravel walking trail. I want to check out the notices tacked to the board, but I know I won't be able to read a damn thing. I pat the base of my throat to see if my reading glasses are hooked on the front of my T-shirt. Nothing.

A quote from Sandy, my *Best Staged Plans* narrator, pops into my head. "The minute life starts getting easier, your eyes go. So the time you once spent looking after your kids is now spent looking for your reading glasses. I hated that."

I hated that, too. Not being able to read without wearing cheaters is one of the few things that really bug me about getting older. I own almost as many pairs of reading glasses as I do notebooks. I scoop up the good ones I find at discount stores and order them online in bulk packages of assorted colors. They're scattered throughout my house and my car and my purses.

And still I can't always find a pair when I need them. So right now I'm thinking I'll try the workaround I sometimes use: close both eyes and then open one quickly, which somehow tricks that eye into being able to read for a second or so. I don't think it's quite what Gauguin meant when he said, "I shut my eyes in order to see," but it's still a handy little trick.

I face the bulletin board and close my eyes. When I open one eye, the print on the notices is clear. Not fuzzy around the edges with a little circle of clear, but really clear. I open my other eye. Whoa. I can read everything.

I can see again! OMG, it's a modern day miracle. Johnny Nash is even serenading me with "I Can See Clearly Now."

One of my hands catches on before my brain does and reaches in the direction of my temple. Okay, so that's where my reading glasses are. Yep, I've been wearing them all along, maybe peering over them as I walked.

A senior moment, you say? I don't think so. I think life has just gotten so crazy complicated that we're completely overloaded with all the things we have to try to remember just to get through the day. So sometimes our head is in about eighteen places at once. We go into autopilot. We get a little bit spacy—or in my case, a lot.

I decide it could have happened to anyone and let myself off the hook. The important thing is to read the bulletin board while I still have my glasses.

I spot a flyer for a drumming circle taking place soon in this very park. I have to admit that the first image that pops into my mind is that brief '90s fad I'd forgotten all about until now. You know, the one where men wandered off to the woods in packs, took off their shirts and beat drums to find themselves. I always wanted to be a fly on that wall. Would it be sexy, in a caveman kind of way? Or would they all turn out to be a bunch of whiners?

In any case, a drumming circle not only sounds like fun, but it's a brand new experience.

I'm in.

Moving On

One of the reasons I decide to write *Best Staged Plans* is to help sell the 1890 Victorian that Jake and I have lived in for 21 years. Sandy, the heroine of that novel, is a home stager, so as I research her world, I not only get some great tips to pass along to my readers, but it motivates me to light a fire under our own downsizing journey.

Thanks to Sandy's expertise, even in a tough market, when we put our house on the market, we have an offer in two-and-a-half weeks. That means we have to find a house fast, so we fly from Boston to Atlanta, look at houses for exactly two days, and make an offer on the one we like best. It needs some work, but we've renovated before. How bad could it be?

Ha. I'm sure there were so many things we could have done differently. We might have stretched our budget and rented a place to live in during at least the first part of the renovation. Or maybe I could have found a tiny office space, or at least learned to work at the library or Starbucks like so many authors do.

But the thing about fixing up a house is that decisions often need to be made on the fly, and being right there for them seems like a big advantage. So Jake and I just move in.

We clean up one of the bedrooms as best we can, blow up an air mattress since we'd ditched our old bed before we moved. We set up my office on a long table at the foot of the air mattress, pile boxes around the perimeter of the room, and let the workmen we hire do their thing in the rest of the house.

We've chosen the house because it's everything our 1890 Victorian wasn't, a '70s ranch with kind of a contemporary feel. There's a back deck that stretches the length of the house, with floor-to-ceiling windows and sliders that open out to the deck. Inside, walls have been knocked down to give the house an open modern layout. There's a sunken living room with a huge double-sided fireplace. The kitchen has tall ceilings and has been renovated with nice stainless steel appliances, plenty of storage, and sleek European-style cabinets.

The bones are there, so the fact that the rest of the house is a pit doesn't really bother us. The first order of business is to get the awful master bedroom and bath stripped down to the studs and reconfigured so we have a sanctuary to escape to.

I'm under deadline with a big New York publisher for a novel, so I don't miss a beat. Every morning we get up early, our backs aching from the stupid squeaky air mattress. Jake finds the dog food for Daisy while I make coffee. We scrounge up something for our own breakfast. I grab another cup of coffee and head back to the dungeon to try to hit my writing groove before the workmen of the day show up.

I write to the sound of circular saws and drills and hammers and men yelling at one another in languages I do and don't understand. I write to the blare of talk radio and to the rhythm of Latin music. Every so often one of the guys appears like a vision to tell me that he wants to write a book, too, and what do I think of this idea. Or to ask me if I'd met Diane Lane on the set of the *Must Love Dogs* movie, and was she just as hot in person?

We've definitely underestimated the ick factor of the room we've moved in to. It has clearly been a teenager's room—

graffiti and stickers decorate the walls, and odd, unidentifiable stains adorn the wall-to-wall carpet. We'd given the walls a quick vacuum and steam-cleaned the carpet. But by the time we realize the room smells profoundly and disgustingly, and maybe ripping out the carpet sooner rather than later might have been a better idea, we have so much stuff piled in the room that it's too late.

One day as I'm opening a window to air things out, a ray of sunlight hits some metal in the window box below. Upon further investigation, I discover a knife, fork and plate buried in the potting soil, perhaps a rebellious teen's way of disposing of the remains of a meal or simply avoiding a trip to the dishwasher.

There's more, lots more, but no need for you to be as grossed out as I was, so I'll just say bugs and decomposing rodents and other creepy things are involved. But we get through it and eventually we move out of that hellhole. Our modestly sized but beautiful master bedroom is finished, complete with a travertine-tiled en suite bathroom with a garden tub and separate shower and dual vanities, as well as a small but decked-out walk-in closet and a cool contemporary paddle fan over our new bed.

It's the first true master bedroom suite we've had in all the decades we've been together. Jake and I move my writing table under our bedroom's big picture window. The view out over the deck to the greenery beyond makes me feel like I'm working in a tree house.

The carpenters move on to the other rooms, one by one. Safe in the new sanctuary, I finish and deliver the first draft of my novel to the muffled sound of disgusting carpet being ripped up and bamboo floors being nail-gunned down. Hollow core doors are replaced with modern solid wood doors. Jake scrapes the popcorn ceilings smooth and paints the walls soothing beachy colors.

Finally, almost a year after moving in, my office is finished.

It's the smallest bedroom in the house, but it has two closets, a great big window, morning light. The walls are painted Sea Salt, a soft sea glass color that looks blue in some lights and green in others.

I'm working on my first set of revisions for the novel now. After the workmen wrap things up, Jake and I rummage for dinner. Then we move my writing table into my new office. We carry in a cool salvage piece we've found—a corner desk with a mid-century vibe—from the garage and arrange a workstation shaped like a U. I roll in my desk chair. We bring in my laptop, my iPhone, my iPad, my printer. My external hard drive backup, my thumb drives, my 12-plug power strip/surge protector. I get everything lined up in a row across the desk and plugged in to the power strip to charge overnight.

I close my eyes, thinking how amazing it's going to be to wake up tomorrow and work in an actual office of my own again.

And then we go to bed, never dreaming that tomorrow will be one of the most devastating days of our lives.

Tough Stuff

So it's my very first day in my brand new office. I start writing just after 5 A.M. I love the early morning quiet, and today I'm beyond thrilled that the noise of construction won't come crashing down on us in a few short hours. Not only do I have a room of my own again, but we have our new house back. All the big-ticket items on this first round of renovations are done, and Jake will be finishing up the rest.

Our son Kaden, who has boomeranged back to live with us for a while, heads off to work. A little before 9 A.M. our daughter Garet, who lives right up the street with our son-in-law Geoff, calls to say she's working remote today and is just about to take the dogs for a quick walk at the nearest park. Do we want to join them? I hear Jake say he and our dog Daisy are in. They'll jump in the car now and swing by to pick up Garet and her dogs.

Normally I'd stay home to get my daily pages done. But today feels celebratory, and since I know I'll have peace and quiet for the rest of the day, I decide to go, too.

Everybody has a busy day ahead so it's a quick walk. The dogs frolic ahead on their retractable leashes while Garet and

Jake and I chat. It's a perfect October day, crisp and almost cool. The leaves make a dry rustle as we walk along the trail.

Not much more than a half hour later, we've dropped Garet and her dogs off and pulled back into our driveway. Jake hands me the keys so I can go in first while he gets Daisy out of the car.

As I reach to unlock our front door, I see that it's not all the way closed. It's a beautiful double contemporary door, and the deadbolt on one side is sticking out. My first thought is that I can't imagine how we could have missed seeing that when we left.

My second thought is that maybe Kaden realized he forgot something when he left this morning, drove back to get it, and in his rush to get to work on time didn't shut the door all the way before locking it.

I push the door open. And then I scream and scream and scream.

Almost nothing in our house is untouched. All those beautiful built-in cabinets have been yanked open, drawers pulled out, contents strewn all over the place. Everything is everywhere it shouldn't be. I spot the contents of my purse scattered on the floor in front of me.

My brain shuts down. I'm numb. Jake is in the house now. We probably should have gone back outside and called the police from there, but we do a slow, tentative walk-through. It doesn't take long to find the break-in point—a floor-to-ceiling contemporary glass panel in the kitchen has been shattered. Glass is everywhere—the floor, the counters, the fireplace hearth, in Daisy's water dish.

We make our way to our bedroom. Daisy is panting. Maybe all three of us are. The pillowcases have been pulled off our pillows. Our new walk-in closet is trashed. Someone has mauled everything, including our underwear, as they pulled it out of the drawers and threw it on the floor. Even though I know whoever did this is gone, I can still feel their adrenaline in this tight space. I can smell remnants of sweat and frenzy.

In the rubble of the closet floor, I spot the clear plastic shoeboxes I'd stored on the top shelves. Before we put our Massachusetts house on the market, I'd gone through every bit of jewelry I'd accumulated over the years, purged as much as I could let go of, and sorted the rest into individual organza drawstring bags I'd ordered in bulk. Then I'd organized all the drawstring bags in the clear boxes to make them easier to move.

The shoeboxes are empty. All my jewelry is gone: the few pieces that had belonged to my mother and grandmothers, everything Jake had ever given me, our wedding rings, cool pieces I'd collected over the years, our daughter's baby bracelets plus both kids' baby teeth, a career's worth of flip-flop and starfish and sea glass jewelry given to me by my wonderful friends and readers to celebrate my beachy books.

I'd even bagged it all up to make it easy for the robbers to dump it into our pillowcases.

When we get to my office, I realize I couldn't have made it easier for someone to grab and go in there, too. The entire row I'd left plugged in, from iBook to iPhone to iPad to external hard drive, is gone. They've even taken my thumb drives and the surge protector. The closet doors have been yanked open and my big canvas bag filled with software is gone.

I no longer have a cellphone, so Jake calls the police with his. We call both kids. Multiple police cruisers show up. A detective asks questions while officers take fingerprints, stomp around the yard, knock on neighbors' doors.

Our daughter arrives and gets right to work calling to cancel my credit cards. She finds out that one of my cards has already been used to fill two vehicles with gas at a station right off the nearest highway. One of the cops heads over there to see if anything has been captured by the gas station's video cameras.

Jake finds his wallet and credit cards in their regular hiding place, undiscovered. The big stuff is still here, too, things like flat screen TVs and stereo equipment.

Our son shows up, checks his room, comes back to report that nothing seems to be missing. *Are you sure?* the detective asks. *It looks like they ripped things apart pretty good in there.* But it turns out that's just the way his room looks, and even though Kaden owns the most valuable electronics in the household, either the robbers never made it to that end of the house, or even they didn't want to venture into his messy room.

I can't stop shaking, and I haven't even realized yet how much I've lost. That my computer backups, and my backups on the backups, have been stolen. That because I'd never gotten around to setting up Dropbox or completely configuring my Mac cloud, the files of all my novels, my interviews, my contacts, my photographs are gone. That because we switched Internet providers when we moved, I won't be able to trace anything through old email attachments.

It hasn't yet hit me that my website files are gone, too, and in order to change even one punctuation mark on my website, I'll have to rebuild the whole thing. I don't have any idea how much time I'll spend Googling myself over the next six months as I try to put the shattered pieces of my midlife career back together again.

And I don't realize how long it will be before I can think about the jewelry. That because my mother died suddenly just before I turned eleven, losing those few tiny pieces I had left of her will feel like losing her all over again. How often I'll wake up with tears running down my cheeks and a sense of loss so powerful that I'd get out of bed to escape it if I weren't now afraid to get out of bed in the middle of the night.

What I do know so far is that I want out. Out of this house. Out of this new life.

Coulda, Woulda, Shoulda

I've never written about the robbery before. It's still hard to talk about it, and right now I really want to put off this section and write about something fun instead.

But bad things happen in the world. Horrible things that you know will stick with you for the rest of your life, even though you have to figure out a way to move beyond them. Bad things happen to good people. To people who aren't perfect but who do most of the right things. To people who aren't reckless.

We like to think we can control these things. That they're not random. That if only we do this, or that, or we don't do this or that, the same kind of bad thing won't happen to us.

Why didn't you have an alarm service? some of these people ask.

Because everyone told us we didn't need one, that this was one of the safest neighborhoods in Metro Atlanta, that even the detective assigned to our case said houses almost never get broken into here.

Do you think it was personal? other people ask. *Do you think they were after your books?*

No, I think they were after small expensive Apple products

that could be quickly wiped clean and sold. If they were after book files, I think they would have robbed Stephen King instead.

Or we get competitive. *That's nothing*, somebody says. *I was robbed three times in one year.*

Or we minimize it. *Oh, well*, somebody else says. *Other than that, how do you like Atlanta?*

The biggest thing I learn from our robbery is that when bad things happen to people, we have the power to make things better or worse for them by what comes out of our mouths when we open them.

I make a vow that when these things happen to other people, I'll listen. I'll let the story be about them and not about me. I won't tell them what they could have or should have done. Or what I would have done, or what once happened, or almost happened, to me.

I'll do the awesome thing and simply say, "I am so sorry that happened to you."

Good Stuff

There's always a bright side. And even though it took me a while to get there after the robbery, eventually I realized how fortunate we were that day.

Even though none of our stuff was ever recovered, the police really tried, the detective stayed in close email contact and treated us with respect. No one was hurt. I wasn't home alone that day writing away. Jake and I hadn't gone out together and left our beloved Daisy, who even at 14 would have tried to protect her turf, home alone.

Our kids and our son-in-law were there for us in a big way, arriving as soon as they could get to us, helping us figure out what needed to be done and jumping in to do it. We couldn't have had a better support team.

After the robbery: It takes Jake and me a while to work up to tackling the mess in our walk-in closet because it feels so personal. For a few days, we keep the closet door shut, opening it just long enough to reach in and grab some clean clothes, which we run through the washer and dryer again before putting them on.

Finally we buck up and start pulling everything out of the closet. As we sort the trampled clothing into piles, I find a few mismatched earrings that must have fallen out of their organza bags on the way to the pillowcase. Somehow losing one earring feels even sadder than losing a pair.

And then my wedding ring rolls across the floor like a gift. Remembering that makes my eyes tear up even now.

I wish I had some magic tip to pass along about getting your life back on track after a traumatic experience. The truth is I just muddle my way through. I wallow long enough to realize that what you focus on becomes your life, and I don't want mine to be about what I've lost. I'm afraid long enough to find out that fear saps the joy right out everything, and obsessing about all the bad things that can happen to you even gets really boring after a while.

Time helps, too. And there's a set point theory of happiness that says we each have a fixed level of happiness that we naturally return to after both good and bad life experiences. So maybe I just start drifting back to my natural pre-robbery happiness level.

But I also remember something one of my fictional characters once said that I've temporarily forgotten: *karma is a boomerang*. When you're struggling, as counterintuitive as it seems, the best way to turn things around is to do something nice for someone else. When you walk through the world with kindness, the world becomes a kinder place. So I start acting like I believe all that until I actually believe it again.

Anyway, eventually Jake and I decide we're not going to let the people who did this to us win. They've disrupted our lives enough. We've already put in an alarm system. We decide to stay in the house we've worked so hard to make ours. The house in the nice neighborhood where nothing bad ever happens until it does.

Getting robbed becomes yet another touchstone. When I have a bad day, I think sure it was tough, but it wasn't as tough as losing someone you love, or going through natural childbirth twice, or finding out a friend has betrayed you. Or getting robbed.

Jake and I limp along for a while until we reach a new normal—more aware, more vigilant, a little bit paranoid. And deeply appreciative of all the good stuff.

Because even though bad things happen to all of us, awesome things happen to us, too, joyful and beautiful and touching and hilarious things. And that's pretty much what keeps you going.

Lavender Fields Forever

I don't know about you, but I could use a dose of lavender right about now.

I first fell in love with lavender while I was writing *The Wildwater Walking Club*. One of the three friends in the novel takes over her family lavender farm, and all three women go on a road trip to a lavender festival in Sequim, Washington, a couple hours northwest of Seattle.

I took a research trip to Sequim during the lavender festival. Seeing and smelling all that lavender blooming at once is truly amazing. Since then I've grown lavender in my own garden, dabbed lavender essential oil on light bulbs, added drops of it to an essential oil diffuser, sprayed lavender water on sheets and pillowcases.

The smell of lavender helps reduce stress and anxiety and even headaches. It can help improve sleep. And it's just a glorious smell. (Unless you're one of those few people that really, really hate the smell of lavender!)

I break out the lavender essential oil, do some Googling, play around with various shower scrub recipes until I come up with this:

Shine On Soothing Lavender Scrub

1 ½ cups Epson salt
1 cup coconut oil
15 drops lavender essential oil
(If you happen to have any, you can sprinkle in a tablespoon or so of dried lavender buds to make it pretty)

Combine all ingredients in a wide-mouth container and stir. Moisturizes and exfoliates. Warning: The bottom of tub or shower will get slippery, so be sure to scrub it off afterward. Also, don't use an Epson salt scrub right after shaving!

Balancing Act

So we've decided we're going to grow awesome instead of old. That we have every intention of shining on and on and on. But even the eternal optimists among us know that everything has a shelf life, and there will come a point when our bodies start inching toward their expiration dates. Obviously, we want to do our best to put off that physical decline as long as possible, say until we're 104 or so.

My plan is to take Dylan Thomas's poetic advice in "Do Not Go Gentle Into That Good Night." I'm going to rave and rage, as he suggests, against that dying of the light.

So I do a bunch more reading to find out what big-ticket items, besides what we eat and how much we move, tend to kick off that downward spiral. Why is it that some people start to seem old in their 30s while others keep sparkling away when they've racked up double and triple those numbers?

It turns out there's plenty of research pointing to the fact that falling is the most serious threat as we age. Sure, we say, but that's eons away, like when we're practically ancient.

I took a tough fall once when I was 31. I was walking to my car at night and my foot caught in a plastic loop that was hooked around some shrubbery. My keys were in one hand,

and I went flying forward with such velocity that when I hit the sidewalk I shattered the radial head of my elbow. I knew immediately it was bad, so I drove myself to the nearest hospital emergency room, trying my hardest not to pass out before I got there. My elbow was the size of a grapefruit when I arrived.

I had a toddler at home as well as an infant I was breastfeeding, so I couldn't even take anything for the pain. And I really needed that elbow—I owned a thriving dance aerobics business with perfect mother's hours. After I explained all this to him, a wonderful orthopedist removed some of the fluid that had built up and shot my elbow full of Novocain to give me some temporary relief from the pain. Then he gave me a removable cast so I didn't have to basically choose between an elbow that straightened and one that bent.

Two days later I started a pretty agonizing course of physical therapy that lasted for five months. My aerobics students organized themselves into a meals-on-wheels brigade and dropped off daily dinners at my house for months, a kindness I will never forget. If I was alone and needed to lift my baby son out of his crib, I had to either grab him by one foot and slide him close enough that I could scoop him up with one arm, or get his three-year-old sister to climb into the crib and help. Eventually I got full mobility of my elbow back, but wow, it was work. And I was young.

There was an older woman I used to see around town. She wore a brace on one leg, which was smaller than the other, and walked with two crutches, the kind with the half circles of metal that wrap around the upper arms. I assumed she'd been unlucky enough to contract polio before the vaccine became available, which I always remember happened the year I was born. And then one day someone told me her story—that in her 20s she'd broken her leg in a skiing accident. Once the cast was removed, she just couldn't push herself past the pain to learn to walk normally. The muscles in her leg atrophied.

And that was it. For the rest of her life, she never walked without her crutches again.

All by way of saying I know how challenging falls can be, and I can only imagine how much truer this becomes the older we get. So if falling's the thing to avoid, what makes us more likely to fall? I flip through a stack of research books and Google away as I try to find the answer.

The experts agree that taking multiple prescription medications considerably ups your chances of falling. I know how fortunate we are to have all these miracle drugs available to us. And yet, the more I read the more I think we sometimes reach for them too soon.

I don't take any medications at all, prescription or otherwise, but I know in my gut that I was well on my way. I'm convinced that if I hadn't begun changing my diet and lifestyle, it was only a matter of time before things like high blood pressure and insulin resistance were my new reality. And from there, who knows.

I keep reading. The next big item on the risk list for falling is balance. It seems pretty obvious that poor balance ups our chances of falling, so I start thinking about things we can do to improve our balance, and maybe have some fun along the way.

Back when I taught kids between the ages of preschool and middle school, one of my favorite things was to invent fun new movement activities for them. I tap into that dormant creativity now and stretch a line of painter's tape down the center of the hallway outside of my office and turn it into a makeshift low-risk balance beam. I pretend I'm a taller but equally perky version of Mary Lou Retton. I extend my arms, flash my pearly whites at the judges, mount my floor-level beam effortlessly. I walk it forward and backward, bending my knees and dipping with each step.

I lean over and extend one leg behind me pretty damn gracefully, if I do say so myself. I go for a 360 pirouette. I start to wobble, but fighter that I am, I reach for the wall on one side of me and hang on to avoid a point deduction.

I walk the length of the pretend beam sideways in both directions—step-slide, step-slide. I extend my arms wide and do ten leg lifts to the front, then to the side, then to the back. I switch sides and repeat. I try it with my eyes closed, which is ridiculously hard, so I decide I'll save upping my difficulty level for my next balance beam routine.

I resist the urge to go for a cartwheel dismount, because I know it won't end well, and simply jump off. I extend my arms in a V for victory. I smile at the judges and wait for my score.

Perfect 10s all around. Awesome.

My faux balance beam routine is a great break from sitting, and it's really fun, too. I realize I've also been working on my balance by using my purple exercise ball as a desk chair. But I have this slight tendency to get carried away, so I want more.

I let my fingers do my shopping online and I learn about balance disks, which remind me of a cross between a low exercise ball and a Frisbee. I find one that's just under twenty dollars. It has nubs on one side so that when you stand on it you can get a foot massage at the same time, which sounds like pretty brilliant multitasking to me. The fact that it's called the HemingWeigh makes it feel almost literary, although I'm not sure Ernest would appreciate the joke.

I move on to the expensive model, the BMW of balance discs. It looks great, too, but just as I'm trying to decide whether to add it to my virtual shopping cart, I realize that for the same money I could finance a gym membership for a couple of months. Which would also ensure that the balance disk didn't ultimately end up tucked away in some corner waiting for me to find somebody to give it to.

I decide to think about it. I roll my trusty purple exercise ball into writing position and get back to work.

Beat It

The Go-Go's are singing "We Got the Beat" to me as I get ready to go to the park for the drumming circle. I tell them they're going to have to knock it off once I start drumming so they don't make me screw up. I have to admit I'm a little bit nervous about making a fool of myself.

Apparently I insult my auditory hallucination, because The Go-Go's disappear and Sonny and Cher show up to sing "The Beat Goes On." Cher's ageless in-your-face cocky confidence is just what I need right now. I join her for the part about how the drums keep pounding a rhythm to your brain. Let's hope.

I've noticed a covered stage in the center of this park, and that's where I'm picturing the drumming circle happening. I'm also imagining a kind of hippy vibe. You know, shirtless men with shoulder-length locks drumming away. Barefoot women in long bohemian skirts and stacks of silver bangle bracelets playing their own drums or dancing around as they shake their maracas or play the tambourine.

Me, I'm dressed for the mosquitos. I'd thought Northern mosquitos were bloodthirsty until I encountered my first Southern skeeters. They're relentless. So if I'm going to be hanging out in a park from dusk into dark, I've decided it's only prudent to wear lined nylon exercise pants, a hoodie over my T-shirt, long socks under my sneakers. Before I even step outside my air-conditioned house to spray on a head-to-toe application of deep woods DEET, I'm sweating. The temperature may be dropping a bit as the sun goes down, but it's still teetering between the 80s and 90s.

It turns out the drumming circle takes place in a wooden gazebo that sits near the edge of the upper parking lot and looks out over the park. It's surrounded by trees, which make the wood structure feel sheltered and semi-private. And of course there's not a mosquito to be found, only a well-sprayed park and an arrangement of citronella candles and lanterns on the floor of the gazebo that some of the drummers have brought in for backup.

Everyone else is dressed for summer in the South—shorts or cropped white pants, nice sandals, sleeveless or short-sleeved shirts. *I'll be right back*, I want to say. And then I'll jump in the car and race home to make a quick change into something a little less ludicrous. But I decide that will only call more attention to my attire, so I just stand there, frozen in place as globs of sweat roll down my back.

Instead of dancing with hippy abandon, the participants are sitting on the built-in benches that edge the inside perimeter of the gazebo. They're all playing instruments—mostly hand drums, but there's also a woman playing a wooden flute, another woman playing the tambourine I imagined, a man playing some egg-shaped shakers.

An assortment of instruments flanks the candles and lanterns. *Help yourself*, someone says in my direction. *Welcome*, someone else says as he slides over on the bench to make room for me. I grab a gourd-like drum that doesn't look too intimidating and sit down. I tap away tentatively.

I glance toward the entrance to the gazebo. A friend has come with me. There's been no arm-twisting—I invited and she said yes. But right now she's leaning back against a high stonewall looking like she'd rather walk barefoot across burning coals than join this drumming circle. I catch her eye and pat the bench beside me. She shakes her head.

A flash of anger hits me. I can understand not wanting to go to a drumming circle. But what I can't understand is going and then just standing there. Why didn't she just say no when I asked her to come with me? I don't want to have to worry about her. I don't want to be responsible for her good time.

And then I realize I don't have to do any of that. She can join us or not. She can walk around the park while I drum. She can ask me for the keys and go pout in my car until I finish.

The guy next to me leans over and tells me I can hit my drum a little harder. I laugh and hit the drum harder, but I'm still feeling pretty shy about it. I love music, but other than a brief stint with violin lessons in fourth grade and an old boyfriend who finally managed to teach me "I Should Have Known Better" on the guitar, playing music has remained one of those elusive things I've always vaguely wished I could do.

My fellow drum circlers don't seem to fit into a single category, unless it's the shared interest in drumming outdoors on a beautiful night. There's a wonderful assortment of people, lots of different ethnic backgrounds, a full range of ages.

Having done my Googling in advance, I pick out the organizer right away. He grew up in Germany in the '60s. An online profile says he loves the way music and dance unite people from around the world.

I take in a couple of twenty-something women who are totally into it. About half the participants seem to have come solo, unless the friends they arrived with are off sulking somewhere. There's a boomer woman over in one corner with a younger man I can tell right away is her son, as well as two granddaughters who also look just like her, and her daughter-in-law.

The guy next to me is great. He's about my son's age, and when I first see him, he's playing a triple set of bongo drums that make me think of Ricky Ricardo. He jumps to another set of drums, and then to some kind of wooden scraper thing. I stop drumming long enough to ask, *Are all these yours?*

Without missing a beat, he tells me that he brought as many as he could fit into his car, but he has lots more at home. He says he's obsessed with buying rhythm instruments and has a tendency to go a bit overboard drum-shopping online late at night. *Here, try this djembe*, he says. He hands me a hand-carved wooden drum, maybe a foot-and-a-half high.

A text beeps into his phone. His thumbs dance as he answers it quickly and then goes back to drumming.

I've done my research on the therapeutic effects of drumming. Drumming reduces our stress and anxiety levels. It helps build our immune system. It's meditative, even spiritual. It's a surprisingly good workout—my poor overworked writer's forearms are really feeling it already. Some soothing kind of mathematical balance seems to be going on in this drum circle, too, as if we're synching both sides of our brains or figuring out some kind of life-affirming equation as we drum.

But the most surprising thing of all to me is that a drumming circle is a conversation. Someone starts a rhythm and then it spreads around the circle as some of the participants repeat the rhythm and others answer it, each in their own way. Even though we're strangers, it's like we know one another on some kind of deep primordial level.

Maybe musicians experience this kind of thing all the time, but as an author I don't get many chances to jam. I'm really glad I've stepped out of my comfort zone enough to do this, and I already know I'll be back.

I drum and drum, staying completely in the moment, which is not something that I manage often. It feels as if time, rather than moving slowly or quickly, is suspended. And then suddenly my first drumming circle is over. Everybody packs up and drifts away.

My friend and I walk across the parking lot. *Sorry*, she says as I click my car doors open. *It's just not who I am.*

I climb into the car, turn my key in the ignition, roll down the windows to let in some fresh air. I can't resist saying, *Don't you mean it's not who you've been so far?*

When we stop for a red light, I turn on the radio. Bonnie Raitt is singing "Meet Me Halfway." I drum along on the steering wheel until the light changes.

I pull into the parking lot where my friend has left her car.

I think I'm going to order a drum so I can practice, she says. *And then maybe next time I'll try it.*

I start to tell her that she doesn't need to practice first. That she's letting perfectionism get the upper hand. She doesn't have to be good at drumming. She just has to loosen up and have some fun.

But one thing I've learned over the years is that it's not up to me to tell my friends how to live their lives. My job is simply to cheer them on.

Good for you, I say.

Starry and Not So Starry Nights

I believe that we're all creative. Some of us have just misplaced this part of ourselves. Embracing our creativity again can be a huge part of shining on.

Picasso said, "Every child is an artist. The problem is staying an artist when you grow up."

I'm not sure what grade I was in when I got the message that the "artistic" kids were the kids who were good at representational art, the ones who could make whatever it was they were drawing or painting look almost as real as a photograph.

"Objective painting is not good painting unless it is good in the abstract sense," Georgia O'Keeffe said. "A hill or tree cannot make a good painting just because it is a hill or tree."

And yet that certainly seemed like what my art teachers were looking for. To my elementary school self, the rule appeared to be that if you could draw a horse, you were artistic. I sucked at drawing horses.

It's a hard thing to shake. I went to a painting on canvas and wine evening recently with some new friends. It was fun to hang out with everybody, and I kept telling myself I was having a blast. As the teacher gave our group of eight midlife women tips on how to make our "Starry Starry Night" paintings look just like Van Gogh's, we all *oohed* and *aahed* over the canvases of the women in our group who copied best. All those old you're-not-an-artist messages bubbled to the surface again.

"I dream of painting and then I paint my dream," Van Gogh said. I think the other thing that was missing for me during our winey painting expedition was that I wanted to paint my own dream, not somebody else's.

Degas said, "Painting is easy when you don't know how, but very difficult when you do." I realize I don't really want to know how. I want to keep this easy breezy. I want to play. I want to find a fun, accessible way to put my own vision on canvas. No worry about technique, no future plans to log what Malcolm Gladwell tells us are the 10,000 hours required to become successful at something.

It's been decades since I've painted anything other than an interior wall or the trim around a window. I flash back to my college days when a friend talks me into taking an art class for non-majors with her because it meets in the evening and she doesn't want to walk across campus alone in the dark.

Even though she's not an art major, she's had a lifetime of art classes and figures the class will boost her grade point average. I'm afraid it might actually pull my own GPA down, but my friend tells me I can always opt to take it pass/fail if I find out I'm in over my head.

The class, which I would never in a million years have taken without some serious arm-twisting, turns out to be fantastic. Our teacher has this great bohemian vibe and a wild head of hair that makes me think of Einstein. We do a series of self-portraits using various media, and I'm totally into it.

And the crazy thing is that the teacher likes my stuff and keeps saying how creative it is. Midway through one class, he holds up one of my self-portraits, flips his hair back dramatically, and says, "I would love to see what you might produce if you spent the next twenty years in the studio."

The end of the semester rolls around. I get an A in the class. My friend gets a B and she's furious. "He just wants to sleep with you," she says.

And even though this seems highly unlikely, especially since the teacher is old enough to be our grandfather and I'm pretty sure he's gay, she hits her mark. I decide something must be wrong with him if he thinks my stuff is good, because I already know I'm not good at art. It will take me many years to learn the other big lesson I missed back then: when a friend needs to put you down, she's not really a friend.

I've held on to a single zippered portfolio since my college days. I have no idea what's in there since I haven't looked at it in forever, maybe even since before I had my kids. I finally find it tucked into the back of a closet in the room where I'd found the purple exercise ball.

The portfolio is mostly filled with old short stories. But surrounded by all the stapled-together carbon copies of typewritten pages, I find a self-portrait I did by scraping a stylus on black scratchboard. I have sunset eyes. Slices of moon make the waves in my hair. A sprinkle of stars shapes one cheek, then travels over my nose to shape the other. It's a sweet, optimistic self-portrait, my own starry, starry night. All these years later, I can see why someone saw promise. Underneath my complete and utter lack of technique and polish was a sparkle of something.

As I hold that scratchboard self-portrait, I have this crazy urge to rock it like a baby.

And then in no time at all I'm in my car and heading for the crafts store, armed with coupons. All I know so far is I don't want to paint small, so I buy a 24-by-36-inch canvas, a bunch of little bottles of acrylic paint, a big brush. Everything's on sale, and with that plus the coupons, I'm out the door again for under twenty dollars.

When I get home, I open the garage door, shake out a drop cloth, flip a wheelbarrow handle-side-up to create a makeshift easel. I know I've got to work fast or I'll start second guessing myself. I rip the plastic covering off the canvas so I can't chicken out and return it.

"Creativity is always a leap of faith," Julia Cameron said. "You're faced with a blank page, blank easel, or an empty stage."

It's been so long since I've done an art project that I briefly consider finger painting. Then I remember how much I love David Bromstad's drippy paintings on HGTV. So I fill a spray bottle with water and drench the canvas. Then I open a plastic paint bottle and squirt some paint on a paper plate. I dab it on the canvas with the brush, spray on some more water, wait to see what happens.

I move on to another paint bottle. I'm using my favorite beachy colors—turquoise and teal and aquamarine. I get a little bit braver and start squirting the paint directly on the canvas.

I swirl together globs of navy and black and white on another paper plate, brush some on the canvas, let that drip down, too. I think my painting might be upside down, so I flip the canvas vertically, spray some more water on it. I decide I liked it better the other way after all, and I flip it back again.

I'm having a blast. It's freeing. It's soothing. It's ridiculously messy. It's seriously therapeutic.

I step back to see what I've got. It looks kind of like a striped beach towel. Intuitively I know that my painting needs some contrast. I grab some bright yellow paint, brush some around at the top of the canvas, reach for my spray bottle.

There it is.

Van Gogh said, "When you hear a voice within you say, 'You cannot paint,' then by all means paint, and that voice will be silenced."

The same goes for singing and drumming and acting and dancing and cake decorating and surfing and knitting and photography and gardening. We don't have to be an expert at things to have a great time doing them.

"While we have the gift of life," Gilda Radner said, "it seems to me the only tragedy is to allow part of us to die—whether it is our spirit, our creativity, or our glorious uniqueness."

My painting reminds me of ever-changing blue skies and the bottomless sea. I decide that because of the splash of yellow sunlight, I can even call it "Shine On."

I don't care what anyone else in the whole wide world thinks of this painting. I think it rocks. I'm going to sign it like an artist and hang it on a wall in my house.

If it ever dries.

Just Write It

I hear from women all the time who've had the same kind of I'm-not-an-artist experience I had with drawing and painting, only about their writing. And it has taken them decades to get back to something they could have been enjoying all along.

If this happened to you, if somewhere along the line you got the message you couldn't write, maybe because your spelling or your grammar or your sentence structure wasn't perfect, or somebody made you feel like you didn't have any talent, I'm so sorry.

And now it's time to shake it off and let it go. To decide to do it anyway.

"There is a fountain of youth," Sophia Loren said. "It is your mind, your talents, the creativity you bring to your life and the lives of the people you love. When you learn to tap this source, you will truly have defeated age."

I've read that 81 percent of people think they have a book in them. Based on my own personal experience, I'd say this number goes up to about 91.9 percent for midlife women. They seek me out at events, find me on Facebook and Twitter, email me through my website after reading one of my books.

I used to feel the responsibility to warn these forty-to-forever women how brutally competitive and market-driven the publishing world is, how slim their chances are of getting traditionally published. And, yeah-yeah-yeah, all that stuff is truer than ever. But when it comes to shining on, I think worrying about those dire publishing statistics is completely missing the point.

Your book could be my drippy painting.

So if writing a book is a buried dream for you, if you have a book you've been carrying around in your heart and soul forever, stop worrying about whether or not you have what it takes to write it. Just write the damn thing.

Move it up on your list of priorities. Maybe even make it number one until you finish it. Start handwriting your first draft in your Shine On notebook, or open up a new file on your computer. Write two pages a day seven days a week the way I do, or come up with your own system. Read or reread *Never Too Late*, where I share lots of advice for writing a book and staying on track.

Maybe you want to write a novel that speaks to other midlife women. Or to middle graders or young adults. Or perhaps it's time to peel back the layers of your personal truth in a memoir. You might want to write a cookbook to preserve your favorite family recipes and make sure they're passed down to the next generation. Or a children's book to welcome your first grandchild into the world. Or a bedtime story for your dog. Or your cats. Maybe you want to revisit a collection of poetry or short stories that you started way back in high school or college.

Do it. Get your story out. Have some fun. Don't overthink it. Don't let your perfectionist tendencies kick in. Let your book take on a life of its own as you write it.

Above all, don't worry about what's going to happen after your book is finished. Just keep going. The discipline of writing day after day, the figuring out how to do it, the digging deep, the creativity, will teach you so much.

Or you'll lose interest along the way and decide that even though you'd love to have *written* a book, you don't want to put in the blood, sweat and words required to actually write one after all. And so you'll find another creative outlet, another way to play. However it works out, you'll have had the courage to try something new.

When you finish your book, you'll have plenty of time to consider your options. A woman I met recently wrote a children's picture book for her grandchild and illustrated it with her own photos. She designed the book herself at an online photo site and now she orders individual copies of it when she needs a baby gift. The book is beautiful and the quality is amazing. You can Google up lots of online options to do this kind of thing.

I know several women who have turned family recipes and stories into cookbook-slash-memoirs, and they give copies to their kids when and if they finally move out. A friend had a book made of the beautiful letters she received from her brother while he was serving time in prison. She gave it to him as a gift when he was released.

When you finish your book, if you decide you want to seek wider publication, you'll research the publishing world and determine whether self-publishing or partner publishing or traditional publishing feels like the best fit for you. You'll educate yourself, do your due diligence, find out everything you can about this new and quickly changing world before you jump in.

Or you'll just pat yourself on the back for finishing a book. As proud as I am of my drippy painting, I have absolutely no interest in entering it in an art show or trying to sell it.

But I sure had fun making it.

Pump It Up

"Life is like riding a bicycle," Einstein said. "To keep your balance you must keep moving."

Move it or lose it, the more contemporary saying goes.

I scroll through my notes again about falling being the thing that's most likely to kick off that downward spiral that leads to old. Once again I'm grateful my recent lifestyle changes seem to be having such a big impact. I'm eating well. I'm moving more. It's not an exaggeration to say that I feel better than I've felt in decades.

I'm also continuing to work on my balance, sitting on my purple exercise ball as I write, and then accessing my inner Mary Lou Retton for a quick balance beam routine on the way to the bathroom or to the kitchen.

But if taking multiple prescription drugs and lack of balance are two of the things most likely to make us fall, I also need to find a way to work on the third component that can keep us from entering that downward spiral—strength.

The experts agree we don't have to grow weaker as we age. We just have to pump some iron or do some other kind of resistance training so we gain muscle and bone density. Strong bones and muscles will keep us moving, give us better posture, make us far less likely to fall off our bicycles, actual or figurative.

Somewhere packed away in the room where my purple exercise ball used to live, I have some exercise bands and handheld weights that I never use. I know either would be a good option to build some strength, and there are plenty of online exercises I can print out to get me going again.

But I decide I should shake things up and actually leave my house instead.

Elvis Costello is singing "Pump it Up" to me while I head out to shop for a gym. There are plenty of local possibilities, so I start with the one closest to home. I'm barely in the door when somebody starts hard-selling membership deals to me. Most of the women working out are wearing makeup and coordinated exercise outfits. They look like they all belong to the same club, one where they don't let you smile.

It takes me a few stops but I finally end up at the YMCA. The people behind the desk are friendly and down-to-earth. The facilities aren't fancy, but there's a nice pool and an indoor track, as well as a great schedule of classes. There are two full circuits of Cybex strength training equipment, a computerized FitLinxx tracking system to keep track of your weight settings and range of motion, Precor stretch trainers. Even balance disks, including the two I'd almost ordered online.

I'm insanely busy trying to keep up with my writing life, taking care of the books I now own as well as writing my next book. But I decide that if I'm going to grow awesome instead of old, this is a gift I need to give to myself. So I join the Y and make a complimentary appointment with a trainer to get up and running on the strength training equipment.

Research shows that two or three strength training sessions each week on non-consecutive days, just one set of 8 to 12 reps working each major muscle group, is all we need to get stronger. To take the pressure off, I decide I'll commit to twice a week, and add a third visit to the gym on the weeks I can make it work. If I have a really workable week, I'll add something like a Zumba class.

I make up a cardio interval routine to do as my warm-up before my strength training circuit: Three laid-back minutes on the elliptical machine. Then twenty seconds as hard as I can. Then a 40 second recovery. I repeat the 20/40-second intervals nine times, upping both the intensity and incline on the machine by one level with each go around. Then I cool down for another three minutes, pedaling backward this time. The whole thing takes just 15 minutes and I'm sweating by the time I finish.

After that I do my strength training circuit—a single set of 8 repetitions at each machine, working up to 12 repetitions as it gets easier. When 12 repetitions starts to feel too easy, I'll add another ½ plate, or 5 pounds of weight, so my muscles will continue to get stronger. (The other way to increase strength is to add more repetitions, but I don't want to put more wear and tear on my joints, and I don't want to add more time to my workout.)

After I finish my strength training, I do some balance exercises on the balance disks, simple things like stepping up, extending one leg, stepping down, then repeating on the other side. After that I do the stretches printed right on the stretch trainer to work on my flexibility. I'm in and out of the gym in just over an hour.

I have a background in fitness. I used to teach dance aerobics many moons ago. I love getting into my zone at the gym, and in many ways it feels just like the zone I get into when I'm writing. I like the physical challenge. I find moving from machine to machine along the strength circuit soothing, even meditative.

And still I had let this part of myself go, and it took me years to get back to the gym again.

One day while I'm finishing up in the stretching room, one

of the trainers walks in with an older couple. They're beautiful—the kind of couple that's been together so long they've started to look alike—but they're so incredibly frail.

The trainer has them sit side-by-side on a wide padded bench and practice standing up without pushing off with their hands. The woman manages three repetitions, the man one.

"Whoa, Nelly Belle," the man says. "This is harder than you'd think."

The trainer tells them not to worry, that they'll take their time and build up their repetitions slowly.

I'm stunned by their feebleness. I can see how easy it would be for them to fall, to break a hip, to get sucked into the vortex of that downward spiral. I make a vow that I will never, ever stop challenging my muscles again.

The trainer tells them that if they want to work on their strength at home, one of the best places to practice standing up without pushing off with your hands is on the toilet seat, since it can't slide out from under you the way a chair might.

They laugh uncomfortably, but I think it's total genius. I decide that at least once a day when I visit the bathroom, I'll hold my elbows and stand up and sit down on the toilet seat ten times. Sure it's a little weird, but I keep doing it until it becomes a habit. And this turns out to be a quick, awesome trick that really works all those big muscles in your lower body.

So if we're ever in the same restroom and it takes me an extra minute to come out of the stall, you'll know what I'm up to!

Every week I see new midlife women at my gym. So many look overwhelmed and uncomfortable in their own bodies, as if they're thinking *how did I let myself get to this point?* Lots of them wear that stereotypical deer-in-the-headlights expression on their faces, like they're afraid everybody in the gym might be staring at them.

But here's one truth I learned way back in my '80s aerobics days: Nobody's looking at you. They're too busy worrying about everyone looking at them.

So be brave. Shop around. Get yourself to a friendly, unintimidating, supportive gym. Keep going until you learn to love it, or at least until you love to hate it.

Or dig up your exercise bands or your handheld weights.

Get yourself strong enough to shine on.

Pumpkin Soup

I'm feeling the urge to get creative in the kitchen. This doesn't happen very often, so I go with it. And this is what I come up with—just in case you're in the mood for soup. (Note: like most soups, it tastes even better the next day.)

Shine On Low Carb Pumpkin Soup

¼ cup coconut oil
4 cloves minced garlic
½ cup chopped onion
1 32-oz. box of chicken broth
2 teaspoons curry powder
1 teaspoon ground coriander
½ teaspoon cinnamon
½ teaspoon nutmeg
1 teaspoon ginger
¼ teaspoon crushed red pepper flakes
pink Himalayan salt to taste
pepper to taste
1 14-oz. can coconut milk

1 15-oz. can pumpkin
pepitas (pumpkin seeds) or walnuts for garnish

1. Melt the coconut oil in soup pot and sauté garlic and onions.
2. Add chicken broth and spices. Bring to boil (I have no idea why, but recipes always say this!) then simmer for 20 minutes or so, stirring occasionally.
3. Stir in coconut milk and pumpkin. Cook for another 10 minutes or so. Taste and adjust seasoning.
4. Top with pepitas or walnuts.

Closet Crash

I've heard about fancy authors who put on mascara and shave their legs and get dressed in actual clothes every day, as if they were going to an office job, before they sit down at their computers to write. But when most of the authors I know are deep in writing mode, it's not a pretty sight.

The T-shirt and sweat pants we slept in morph into the ones that we write in or walk in or wear to the grocery store or to the gym. And sometimes all of the above. I even know one prolific author who psyches herself up—and grosses out her family—by pulling on a big baggy sweatshirt as she goes into the home stretch of a book and not taking it off again until she finishes writing the final page.

All by way of explaining that even though I might have vaguely noticed that I was yanking up my yoga pants a lot more and that my baggy T-shirts were getting baggier, most of my head is in the book I'm writing. And so I really don't realize the degree to which my clothes no longer fit until I start rummaging through my closet for something to wear to teach an upcoming reinvention workshop.

I try on one of my go-to outfits. When I give the bottom half a little yank, it slides right down over my hips. It seems beyond ironic that when I finally focus on feeling better, the extra weight comes off without even trying. I wonder randomly if there might be a reverse parallel for writing a book, something I could do that would allow me to check my daily pages one day and find out that the word count had multiplied exponentially while I was doing something else, like maybe sleeping.

And then I just skip merrily into denial. I eyeball a few tops and decide they'll probably still fit. I'm pretty sure there's a jacket or two I might be able to sneak by with. And if I wash one of the gazillion pairs of black pants I own in scalding water and give them an extra-long spin in a hot dryer, I'll be good to go.

Fortunately, right around this time my daughter happens to stop by for something on her way home from work. I ask her for a quick consult on the outfit I'm planning to wear to the workshop. I dash to my closet, make my best guess, put it on.

When I return, my stylishly dressed daughter looks me up and down.

"You're kidding, right?" she says.

Okay, so clearly I've got some work to do. The experts agree that the best way to do a complete wardrobe overhaul is to pull all your clothes out of your closet and try them on.

I find a quote by the fabulous Stacy London to inspire me: "Your closet needs to be a place of joy and celebration of who you are now—not who you were."

Marie Kondo, author of *The Life-Changing Magic of Tidying Up*, concurs. She advises us to hold each item and ask, "Does it spark joy?"

Joy seems like a great collective theme, but my closet still sometimes feels like a crime scene to me, so I've got a long way to go to get there. I wonder briefly if I should start with a quick exorcism or sage smudging, but decide my best bet is to stay focused.

So I pile all my clothing on my bed—tops on one side, bottoms on the other, hybrids and miscellaneous items in the middle. Along one wall I arrange my shoes, a couple pairs of boots, the crazy number of flip-flops I've accumulated over the years.

I channel Sandy, my home staging heroine from *Best Staged Plans*, who tells me to separate everything into three piles: DUMP, DONATE and KEEP. I decide I need more categories to survive this, so I add SENTIMENTAL and SECOND OPINION.

I find a beautifully made formal dress that was my mother's mixed in with my clothing. I discover some monogrammed handkerchiefs, embroidered by French nuns for my maternal grandmother, which were given to me because we share the same three initials. A couple of dresses I wore for special things like the *Must Love Dogs* movie premiere, some T-shirts from long ago vacations and trips that would probably turn to dust if I tried to pull them over my head. Some things I haven't worn in forever with interesting details like cool beading. A few extra-funky pairs of flip-flops.

That's it. These are the things I want to hold on to. They connect me to my past, inform who I am today, link me to my future. I find room in an old cedar chest for the entire sentimental pile. Now that it's all in one place, I can visit this stuff whenever I want to. But I think it'll be easier for me to figure out what to wear if my closet is about the clothes I actually use and not about memories.

I try on everything that's left. The clothes that still have price tags on them make me cringe. I shake my head at the solo pieces I loved enough to buy but could never find anything to go with.

And pretty much nothing fits. This is beyond editing a wardrobe—it's more like deleting one. It's both freeing and overwhelming at the same time.

What helps me let it all go is imagining these clothes

bringing joy to other women when I donate them rather than let them rot in my closet. I gave the keynote at the International Dress for Success conference a few years ago, so even though I don't own much in the way of business attire, I earmark some jackets and pants a woman returning to work could rock on a job interview Dress for Success sets up for her. I Google up some area women's shelters and the nearest Goodwill for the rest.

Then I change into a fresh baggy T-shirt and yank up my yoga pants.

Digging in the Dirt

I'm having one of those days. There are a gazillion things I need to do and I can't seem to get to any of them. My house is a pit. My inbox is overflowing with email that I really need to answer. Every time I turn on the TV or check social media, I feel battered by all the negativity out there in the world.

When announcing the Oscar winners in the best screenplay categories one year, Robert De Niro said, "The mind of a writer can be a truly terrifying thing. Isolated, neurotic, caffeine-addled, crippled by procrastination, consumed by feelings of panic, self-loathing, and soul-crushing inadequacy. And that's on a good day."

The fact that one of my Twitter followers recently tweeted this quote feels like an omen. My hard-earned positivity flies right out the nearest window. I mean, why even bother to write my daily pages? I start to wonder if I have anything left to say. If I'll ever finish another book. And even if I do manage to finish one, if it will turn out to be pathetic, as opposed to the amazing book I should have written.

Maybe I should just hang it up and try to get a job at Trader Joe's instead. Maybe I'd get a discount on coconut oil.

I white-knuckle my way through my daily pages, fighting

self-sabotage every step of the way. I know if I let myself off the hook today, it will be that much easier to skip those pages tomorrow. And the next day.

Finally my two pages are finished. Time to get out of my head. I shut down my computer and cell phone, pace a few aimless laps around my house.

"If you have a garden and a library, you have everything you need," Cicero said.

Although disappearing into a good book usually cures just about everything for me, today I'm beyond bibliotherapy. But my garden has been calling out to me for a while now, and I've been ignoring it.

I douse myself with sunscreen and slip into my rubber gardening clogs. I find my sunglasses and stand on the porch as I spray on some mosquito repellent.

I make myself weed with both hands, so I'm challenging my brain as well as my muscles by using my non-dominant side. I bend from my knees to save my back.

There's nothing more humbling than weeding—it's impossible to be full of yourself while you're doing it. Weeding also keeps us focused on the now. It's tenacity in action. It starts to feel like anything is possible if we just hang in. As I weed and weed and weed, I can feel my doubts fading away.

A big southern magnolia is just coming into bloom, and the breeze carries the lemon-crossed-with-vanilla scent over to me. The sweet unmistakable smell of honeysuckle follows right behind it. I walk across my front yard to take a sniff of the pink tea rose that always smells like tea to me.

"The best things in life are nearest," Robert Louis Stevenson said. "Breath in your nostrils, light in your eyes, flowers at your feet."

I shovel up a huge clump of iris that's just past bloom. I divide it into sections, replant about a third, bag up the rest to give away. Rich clay soil covers my gardening gloves like a second set of gloves.

The rhythmic pecking of a woodpecker high up in a pine tree keeps me company. It's a kind of drumming, with a cadence all its own, and I know this is the way woodpeckers establish territories and attract mates. I look up, but I can't find it. I drum on the nearest tree trunk with the handle of my shovel, trying to repeat the pattern back to the woodpecker. I hear a series of shrieks and then more pecking, faster this time.

"Sorry, but I've already got a mate," I say in case I accidentally sent it the wrong message. "Thanks anyway though." I look over my shoulder to make sure my next-door neighbor isn't watching me talk to an unseen woodpecker.

I go back to weeding. I look up as a chipmunk darts across the lawn and disappears under the front porch. I divide some Lenten roses and make a swooping pattern with them under the shade of a Japanese maple.

Our gardens can reflect our personalities—formal or wild, colorful or tranquil—and give us yet another way to cultivate our creativity. Gardening forces us to unplug, reminds us to keep it simple. It engages our senses and makes our brain forge new connections. Several studies have shown that those who garden regularly have a lower risk of dementia than non-gardeners.

You don't even need to have your own garden to reap the benefits. Just wandering through a garden center and breathing in the warm, moist air of the greenhouses while checking out all the plants can lower your stress levels and lift your moods.

"Flowers are restful to look at," Freud said. "They have neither emotions nor conflicts."

Community gardens are a great way to learn about gardening or connect with like-minded people while digging in the dirt. My friend Katya missed her garden after downsizing from a house to a condo, so she volunteers at a food bank garden that has donated 10 tons of produce to a food pantry over the years.

Botanical gardens are among the most magical places in the world, and an awesome way to fit in a walk when you're traveling. I've visited terrific botanical gardens in Denver and St. Louis while on book tour. Atlanta Botanical Garden has a great 600-foot long canopy walk, plus an incredible collection of orchids. Massachusetts has a consortium of botanic gardens, including Arnold Arboretum, which hosts one of my favorite events, Lilac Sunday, when hundreds of lilacs are in bloom.

Chicago Botanic Gardens has a huge collection of bonsai. Fairchild Botanic Gardens in Coral Gables, Florida, has fabulous cacao and vanilla orchards, and San Francisco Botanical Gardens has an amazing collection of magnolias.

Canada's Montreal Botanical Garden has Chinese and Japanese gardens and a First Nations Garden. The 300-acre Royal Botanic Gardens in Kew, England has the world's largest collection of plants. Berlin-Dahlem Botanical Gardens in Berlin, Germany has a cactus pavilion as well as a pavilion housing orchids and water lilies. When I spoke at a literary festival in Denmark, I found time for a peaceful bog and butterfly-filled walk through Aarhus Botanical Gardens near Old Town.

I shake my head to bring me back to my own garden. Just a few hours after walking away from everything that was bringing me down, I'm filthy and exhausted. But my garden looks great. And I remember who I am.

"A garden is the best alternative therapy," Germaine Greer said.

Checking In

I ask the midlife women hanging out on my Facebook author page this: *If nothing was standing in your way, what new thing or things would you like to learn or do?*

Nancy would climb a mountain. Kabuki would live in Italy, teaching English and learning Italian. Lisa would restore an old house with secret passages. Meredith would fix houses in low-income urban areas and find a way to give them away. Joyce would learn quilting. Debbi would go to law school to study intellectual property law. Leslie would open a thrift store. Hailey would sky dive. Hope would teach astronomy.

Allison would become a lifetime student and just keep learning. Jean would start fresh and live exactly the way she wants where she wants. Katy would paint, draw and travel. Cathy would become an accomplished baker. Suzanne would learn sign language. Pam would relearn French.

Sheilah would have a hot dog cart. Dawn would try parasailing. Judi would take art lessons. Jenna would play an instrument. Donna would refinish furniture. Terri would work with mentally challenged children and adults.

Charlene would try stand-up comedy. Beth would try paddle boarding. Sheila would play the piano. Katherine would learn landscape design. Sabre would learn to paint. Ali would learn a new language. Sharon would travel and take photographs. Rita would try roller-skating.

What strikes me is how eminently doable most of these things are.

"Nothing happens unless first we dream," Carl Sandburg said.

"Without leaps of imagination, or dreaming," Gloria Steinem said, "we lose the excitement of possibilities. Dreaming, after all, is a form of planning."

But one thing I've learned on my own journey is that the only way to go from dream to reality is to take action.

The first step is to get clear on whether or not you really want to do it. If you do, commit to it. Write it on a fresh page in your Shine On notebook. Make it a goal and figure out how to get there. For instance, Allison's page might look something like this:

New Thing: Become a Lifetime Student and Keep Learning

1. Make a list of things I'd like to learn.
2. Investigate sites like openculture.com for free online courses. Check out YouTube for free video tutorials.
3. Google continuing education classes in my area, and commit to taking one class per quarter.
4. Photocopy this page and tape it to my bathroom mirror where I'll see it first thing every morning.

Okay, your turn.

New Thing:

1.
2.
3.

4.

This might be a good time to flip back in your notebook to find your original Shine On List—the 5 things you know so far that will lead you to awesome.

Should your New Thing become the new #1 on that list? You can rework your list on the next page and in your Shine On notebook:

Shine On List: 5 Things That Will Lead Me to Awesome

1.
2.
3.
4.
5.

Second Opinion

The fashion experts agree about the transformative power of clothing. Upgrading the way we dress can boost our confidence and self-esteem. It can be a potent anti-depressant. A wardrobe reinvention helps others see us in a fresh light, which can attract all sorts of cool new opportunities into our lives.

My daughter Garet stops by again so I can try on my second opinion clothes for her. She rules out most of them. The blouse I know is too big now but I'd hoped might be long enough that I could get away with wearing it as a tunic. My all-time favorite denim jacket—when she points this out, I have to agree that it does hang kind of shapelessly now.

So I bag up most of the second opinion clothes, too. For years I've opened my closet and felt like I didn't have a thing to wear. Now I really don't.

Nobody tells you the truth like a daughter. And while that can certainly be a double-edge sword on occasion, if you're lucky enough to have a daughter who knows her fashion, understands the difference between what works for her and what works for you, and just so happens to live nearby, it's a huge advantage.

By midlife, many of us need someone to tell us that the '90s called and wants those mom jeans back. Or the '80s. Or even the '70s. We've been looking at our closets for so long it's difficult to really see the stuff in them. It's also hard to see ourselves clearly, because the way we look now gets all mixed up with the way we used to look and how young we still feel inside. If we've lost, or gained, a bunch of weight, then we need another set of eyes even more.

If you don't have a fashionista daughter you can bring in, you can ask a friend who's rocking her midlife look. Some department stores offer free personal shoppers and promise not to pressure you to buy. Or you can Google up a freelance stylist or wardrobe consultant to hire, or ask around to see if anyone you know has had a good experience with someone and can give you a referral.

You can make friends with that savvy, stylish midlife woman who hands out the dressing room tickets at Marshall's. Or the owner of a local boutique. A woman I know tries on her clothing, takes a selfie with her phone, and texts it to her son's girlfriend. If *not my favorite look* comes back, she knows it's time to ditch the outfit.

It's important to find the right wardrobe fairy godmother. You don't want a sales person who tells you that every single thing you try on looks great because she's working on commission. You need honesty, but you don't want to expose yourself to someone who won't leave you feeling fabulous and empowered. You also don't want to end up looking like a clone of that friend or stylist who looks amazing but whose taste, personality, and lifestyle are completely different from yours.

Because the more I read the more I realize it's really about finding a look that matches who we are now as well as who we want to be as we move forward. It's about finding a look that will help us shine on.

Signature Look

One thing I know for sure is that I've reached the place in my life where I'm over having lots of stuff. Letting go of most of my clothes is a great excuse to simplify.

Because our lives are all so different, we each have our own unique clothing challenges. As an author, I spend most of my time wearing scruffy clothes that no one ever sees, which I think of fondly as my writing pajamas. Then I venture out into the real world to speak or to teach. And not only do people see me then, but photos turn up, especially on Facebook. I don't really need or want to own lots of clothing, but if I wear the same thing repeatedly, it doesn't take long for it to look like, *Will somebody please buy that poor author some new clothes?*

I once read that the average woman spends an entire year of her life trying to decide what to wear. I want to spend that time on other things. So my theory, after much time spent on Pinterest and some serious fashion blog research, is that what I need to do is start with some basic neutral foundation pieces—a uniform of sorts—things I can wear again and again and that will essentially disappear in the photos.

But first I have to figure out what size I am. So after I

finish writing for the day, I head out to shop. I make a wild guess to get started, but it takes me several trips to the dressing room to realize I've dropped at least three full sizes.

And wow, what a difference the right fit makes. I realize that even before I lost weight I'd been wearing my clothes too big for years, hoping they'd be more forgiving.

I find an updated pair of slim pants that fits perfectly and has just enough stretch to be comfy. So I buy the pants in three colors—black, white and cobalt blue. I'm not sure the blue counts as a neutral, but I love it, so too bad. I buy coordinating tanks for layering as well as a couple of dressier sleeveless tops that float away from all the places I don't want to call attention to.

Everything's on sale and I've also got coupons, so it doesn't even cost all that much. And it completely changes my life. Whenever I need to go somewhere, I mix and match these few pieces instead of standing there agonizing over what to wear.

Then I layer on something with sleeves—a jacket or blouse or cardigan or wrap or poncho or duster. Again, what a difference the right fit makes.

I don't want to get too cookie cutter, so I Claire-ify my look with fun things that speak to me. Cool scarves that I've collected over the years—I Google up some scarf videos and find fun new ways to tie them. Silver jewelry—nothing valuable for me ever again, just funky statement pieces. A bag with retro fringe. A wristlet clutch with metal studs. I don't want to look like anyone else. I'm not competing with anybody. I want to be unique and authentically who I am.

I've spent enough time online by now to know that heels can do a lot for your legs, but by midlife we know what we're over, and I'm seriously over heels. Unless maybe I'm sitting down and someone walks a pair over to me. So I watch the sales and buy flats with arch support in black, nude, and cornflower blue. They're all comfortable, and one pair even has memory foam soles—bonus!

My daughter weighs in to warn me that I'll look dated if I get too matchy-matchy with my accessories. I learn to add one pop of color, not two. To edit my statement jewelry down to one big piece. Not to match my shoes and my purse—although I'm relieved to learn that at least my shoes are still allowed to match each other.

I spend some joyful hours making outfits as if I were playing dress-up, which I guess technically I am. When I come up with a good look, I have someone take a photo or I take a selfie so I don't forget how I did it. I order some prints of the photos online for future reference and tuck them into my Shine On notebook.

Eventually I'll add a few more basics, upgrade my exercise wear, find a great pair or two of jeans. Maybe someday I'll even update my writing pajamas, though that might be getting a bit too carried away. But I vow that I'll never again buy anything that I don't really love, especially just because it's on sale.

I learn what works for me and where to find it. I can cruise through Marshall's in five minutes flat to see if anything has my name on it. I check Steinmart, Chico's, Nordstrom Rack, a local boutique or two. I watch Hoda and Kathie Lee's Ambush Makeovers on the *Today Show* and fall madly in love with Clara Sunwoo clothing, the perfect funky midlife look I'm going for.

My fashion reinvention is surprisingly fun. It's like being my own canvas, as if I'm painting my outside to make it a better match for my inside. A way of saying this is who I am and what I bring to the world. I've never really had that passion for fashion, or even quite understood the whole clothes thing before, so this experience is all new for me, a complete epiphany. It's another way of being creative.

I'm not sure I would have taken it on if I hadn't lost the weight, but I absolutely should have.

When I show up to teach my reinvention workshop, the

first midlife woman who comes up to me says, "You look just like an author."

"Cool," I say. "That's exactly what I was going for."

Signing On

My drippy painting is actually dry! Time to sign it and hang it up.

But first I decide I need some signature inspiration. Maybe I'll take a field trip to an art museum. Or attend an art show featuring a local artist. So I start Googling up some possibilities.

And I find out Peter Max is coming to town for a traveling exhibit. The Peter Max. I love his bold, bright, trippy, psychedelic '60s pop art, pieces like "Cosmic Runner," as well as some of his later neo expressionistic work. I even owned orange and yellow Peter Max stationery when I was in high school.

I ask my husband if he wants to come with me.

"He's still alive?" Jake says.

"Give him a break," I say. "He's only 77."

And it turns out Peter Max is a great example of growing awesome instead of old. He spends 10 to 12 hours a day doing what he loves. His work can be found in over 2000 galleries and art museums in the world. He's even created artwork for *The Voice*.

The exhibit takes place on a rainy night. It's everything I can do to stay awake for it. But I'm so glad I do. It's just the reminder I need that creativity is a huge part of shining on.

"All day long, I'm creative," Peter Max has said, "and the second I get a little tired of any given medium, I just shut that area down and go to the next room. I just go do something else."

I'm totally inspired. I meet Peter Max. Jake takes my picture in front of one of his paintings. Then I sneak around and take pictures of Peter Max's signature on several of his other paintings in the exhibit. I'm relieved to find out his signature isn't even that complicated, just a thickly painted *Max* with the horizontal line of the *A* becoming one leg of the *X*.

"I told you he was alive," I say to Jake as we walk back into the rainy night.

When I've finished my pages the next day, I open my Shine On notebook and start doodling my own signature. I haven't done this since high school, when I used to write my name over and over again in a notebook a lot like this one. I wrote my name in bubble letters. I wrote it backwards in mirror writing. I wrote it with a circle or a heart or a star dotting the *i* in *Claire*.

I don't think I realized it back then, but as I worked on my signature I was trying to figure out who I was and how I wanted the world to see me.

Just before my first book was published, I practiced signing my name again. How did other authors sign their names? Which page of the book was I even supposed to sign anyway? Should I write my name in an illegible scrawl so I'd look like a more literary author? Should I sign it really big to make my book seem more important? Or small, so I don't set up any false expectations?

In the end, I simply sign my name, grateful to get to keep

signing it with each new book. Once, after I sign a book for a reader who has studied handwriting analysis, she tells me that my signature says that I'm both highly creative and highly diplomatic.

"What the hell is that supposed to mean?" I say, and fortunately she gets my not-so-diplomatic joke and laughs.

But what I realize as I continue to sign books is that the whole thing is really more about the person I'm signing the book for than it is about me. It's an opportunity to connect with someone who's giving me the gift of my midlife career. So I focus on inscribing the book to this wonderful reader and saying something personal. You can't take the former teacher out of the author, so I also have custom stamps made for most of my books—a dog print for *Must Love Dogs*, a flip-flop for *Life's a Beach*—to accompany my signature and make it more special.

Right now I'm kind of wishing I'd thought to have a stamp made with my signature on it so I could just press it onto the lower right-hand corner of my drippy painting and be done with it. I know it's ridiculous, but I'm totally intimidated by the thought of signing it.

I find a thin brush, which is actually a makeup brush, but you work with what you've got. I briefly consider continuing the theme by signing my painting with an ancient pot of gel eyeliner that I never mastered. But with my luck the eyeliner would turn out to be waterproof, and if I screw up my signature, I'll end up with a permanent blob. So instead I squirt some black acrylic paint on a paper plate.

I practice my makeup brush signature on a fresh page of my notebook, over and over again. Then I rest my drippy painting on a long table in my office so the paint won't run. I take a few deep breaths.

Claire Cook isn't exactly a hard name to sign. It doesn't even have a single letter that dips below the line to get fancy with.

But still it takes me almost as long to work up to signing my painting as it did to paint it.

Finally, I go for it and just sign the damn thing.

My signature isn't perfect or impressive, but it's mine. And now after all these years, in my mind, which is the only place that really counts, I'm officially one of the artistic kids.

Hair We Are

I find the perfect spot for my signed painting. It's just past my imaginary balance beam area, at the end of the hallway. I decide I'll try to think of this hallway as *the gallery* from this point forward.

But of course the thing about life is that just when you think you've got part of it figured out, right around the corner another challenge pops up. I head out again by way of the Atlanta airport, this time to give the keynote at Women's Wellness Day in Rhode Island.

Usually I fly with just a carry-on, but this trip links to another one, so I check a bag at Delta curbside.

The baggage guy looks at my license. "You've made some changes since that last picture."

I hope he means that as a compliment. "Thanks," I say.

He takes another look at my driver's license, then at me.

"You've got some flavor going on, Ms. Cook. Looking good."

I thank him again, resist the urge to get all needy and add, *Do you really think so?*

A woman edges in next to me with her suitcase. She's maybe my age, maybe a few years younger, with brown hair that's clearly been dyed and is pretty close to the shade my hair used to be colored.

"My mother was 85 before she got her first gray hair," she says to the baggage guy. Like I can't hear her.

The baggage guy ignores her. I scratch my cheek in her direction with my middle finger so he can see it but she can't, and he cracks up.

"You're still in the game," he says as he takes my suitcase.

Sure he's working for a tip. And he totally deserves one.

I tell the whole story of my hair reinvention in *Never Too Late*, but in a nutshell, after covering the gray for years and years, my hair became increasingly resistant to dye. So eventually I decided to let it be the color it wanted to be.

Our hair's a big deal. Whether we love it or struggle with it, our hair says a lot about us, and a bad hair day can really throw us off. My transition to au natural included quite a few of those bad hair days, plus a fair amount of hiding out, an ugly knit hat, a couple of ombre phases, a short-short haircut, a few lowlights, a supportive hair stylist. (Thank you, Rhonda Johnson!) It took about a year or so and it wasn't always easy, but I'm so glad I did it.

But I didn't expect that the gray hair thing would turn out to be such a lightning rod issue. Not only does everyone have an opinion, but some women even interpret my decision not to dye as some kind of judgment on their decision to dye. They tell me they'd never do what I've done. They say they've heard that gray hair makes you look 15 years older. Somebody recently left this comment on a Facebook photo of me: *That's such a great picture I almost didn't notice the gray!*

Just for the record, it's your hair and I think it should be any color you want it to be. Be blonde! Go blue! Whatever works for you!

But lots of other women reach out to thank me for giving them the courage to stop dyeing their own hair, something they've wanted to do for years. Which is really, really cool.

I love that silver is the new black, that it's becoming cutting edge, pun intended. I'm thrilled that gray is now okay, and by any name you want to call it: pewter, sterling, even arctic blond. I don't think gray hair makes us look 15 years older. In fact, I think the way nature softens our looks with those wisdom highlights, those strands of midlife tinsel, is like draping a scarf over a bright light so it's not too harsh on our features. I think it can make us look stunning.

I even think the process is fascinating. I had no idea that we usually go gray front to back. Right now my hair is mostly salt and pepper, but the front is lighter, some of it pure white.

DeBarge jumps out of 1982 to sing "And I Like It." I'm thrilled they like the way I comb my hair and the stylish clothes I wear, but I'd be okay even if they didn't. That's a pretty awesome feeling.

My gray hair makes me feel as if I know who I am and I'm not hiding anything. I love that I'm no longer a slave to my demanding roots—at the risk of overstating it, this is what freedom means to me. Most of all, my new hair makes me feel like a midlife rebel. Brave and independent and authentic.

Rocking' the Silvah

If you decide to join the silvah sistahood, it's important to find a hair stylist who will support you. (There's also a Gray and Proud group on Facebook you can join.) An updated, stylish cut is key to pulling off gray. We want it to look intentional, as opposed to like we've let ourselves go. (Especially if the transition includes a serious skunk stripe like the one I had going on for a while there!)

As I was researching this section, I kept stumbling on all these dire warnings about gray hair being bone dry, wiry, coarse, frizzy. As if these things will all go away if you cover up the gray. Sure our hair is dryer now, whether we dye it or not, but what isn't? We just have to learn to work with it.

When I wrote *Summer Blowout*, my novel about a pseudo-Italian Irish-American family of hair salon owners, I shadowed some fabulous real life hair stylists and makeup artists as part of my research. Readers always tell me that they got some great beauty advice from that book and often thank me for naming actual products. So just in case it's helpful to you, I'll share a few of the things I've been using on my own gray hair journey.

Since my hair is dryer now, I don't wash it as often as I

used to. Maybe twice a week I use L'Oreal EverCurl sulfate-free shampoo and conditioner. Once a week I use a purple shampoo first, lately Jhirmack Distinctions Silver Plus, which I find works just as well as the more expensive violet shampoos for me (they're all kind of harsh, so make sure you don't use them more often than once a week), to get rid of any yellowing and to make the white whiter.

To add more shine and keep my gray hair from looking dull, I warm the tiniest bit of coconut oil by rubbing it between my hands, and then I rub my hands over my hair. (This is essentially my leave-in conditioner.) I don't use argan oil, or anything else that has a yellowish tint, because I don't want my white hair to pick up the yellow.

Before I wash my hair, I add a more generous application of coconut oil and leave it on for a few hours or even overnight. (If coconut oil's not your thing, Neutrogena Triple Moisture Deep Recovery Hair Mask works well, too.)

To add even more shine, once a week I use John Frieda Luminous Color Glaze Clear Shine on my dry hair before I wash it. The directions say 20 minutes, but I have a tendency to forget and leave it on until I finish my daily pages, and so far that's worked out fine.

My hair has gotten not only healthier, but curlier since I stopped having it colored. So I decided to embrace the curl, too, and ditch my blow dryer. Now I just work some John Frieda Frizz-Ease Curl Reviver Mousse (silicone-based to lock out the frizz) into my wet hair. After that I spray on a little John Frieda Dream Curls Daily Styling Spray. There are plenty of great products out there at all price points, and I've tried lots of them (research!), but right now these are the two I keep going back to. When I'm in the mood for crisper rather than softer curls, sometimes I use TIGI Catwalk Curls Rock Amplifier instead of the Dream Curls.

Then I turn my head upside down, scrunch my curls with my hands, flip my head back up, and let my hair air-dry. I've found that the less I touch it as it dries, the more likely my hair is to dry curly and frizz-free.

In the morning when I wake up, I spritz on a little more Dream Curls Daily Styling Spray and give my hair another upside down scrunch, which restores the curls.

If I need my hair to stay put, I use Paul Mitchell's Freeze and Shine Super Spray, which even comes in a travel size.

Lou Reed jumps in to serenade me with "Walk on the Wild Side," which reminds me that when I need my own little walk on the wild side, I use ColorMe by Giuliano temporary hair mascaras to paint on a few streaks of bright color. Blueberry is my favorite, but there are lots more, from Tangerine to Violet Night to Red Rush. They're inexpensive, they really cover, and then they wash right out when you're over them.

Using hair mascara makes me think of those old mood rings from high school that were supposed to change color based on the way we were feeling. So it's a little bit retro, a little bit rebellious, but mostly, it's fun!

Other Shades of Shining

Just in case neither gray hair nor hair mascara is your thing, I reached out to my hair stylist friends to ask what the rest of us can do to make our hair shine on. They all agreed that letting our hair get too dark is the biggest mistake women make as the years go by, because it really ages us. So watch out for sliding into that shoe polish look—flat, one-dimensional single process color that just keeps getting darker and darker with every application. Basically, lighten up! And think about going brighter, too, by adding some highlights to break up that solid block of color.

Beyond that, the hair experts agree that we should shake things up once in a while so our hairstyle stays current. I love change, so I have to admit I've overdone this a few times with overly trendy haircuts, something that becomes pretty apparent in hindsight when those old photos resurface. But not every risk pays off, and hair grows back. And at least I had the guts to go for it, as opposed to keeping the same cut I've had since high school. (Which in my case was so not worth keeping.)

Another tip from the experts: Watch out for helmet hair—

that all-one-piece matronly look. Texture and layers add movement, and that's what we're going for.

If you're learning how to embrace your naturally curly hair like I am, know that as your hair dries there can be a shrinkage factor of up to four inches. (If that just triggered a *Seinfeld* episode flashback, you're not alone!) So watch out that your layers don't get too short at the top, or when your hair dries, you could end up looking like a French poodle. (Lesson learned!)

The conventional wisdom used to be that as women age, our hair should go shorter. I think a short, stylish haircut can make us look confident and totally awesome. But I also see lots of women who are rocking their long, gorgeous, healthy, vibrant hair at midlife. The experts I spoke to say we shouldn't let our hair grow longer than just above our shoulders, because it will drag our features down. But there's an exception to every rule, and bottom line, it's our hair and we should wear it any way we want to.

As Emerson said, "To be yourself in a world that is constantly trying to make you something else is the greatest accomplishment."

Catitude and Gratitude

So I'm back on a plane, heading to my next speaking gig. Once I'm settled in my seat, I open my iPad and take another look at the answers to the Facebook question I've posted: *If nothing was standing in your way, what new thing or things would you like to learn or do?*

Jodi would work with animals in some capacity. Georgette would buy a ranch and take in all the old and disabled animals she could so they could have peaceful, restful days. Malina would work with search and rescue dogs. Christina would open a retirement home for cats and dogs. Debby would train therapy dogs. Joan would help relocate shelter cats to nursing homes and assisted living centers. Candy would start a sanctuary farm where animals and addicts in recovery could rescue one another.

Oh, I hope they do it. I hope these awesome women get clear on their goals, commit to them, figure out how to achieve them, take action. I can't imagine a better way to shine on.

There's a woman I see at one of my new favorite walking places, a 3½-mile trail along the river, who always carries a small plastic container filled with treats to give to the dogs she passes. She's been doing this for 26 years. I love watching how giving out these goodies boomerangs back to this midlife woman. Both canines and humans treat her like she's the belle of the trail.

"Dogs are not our whole life, but they make our lives whole." Roger Caras said.

Several women I know volunteer at animal shelters—answering phones, walking dogs, fundraising. Not only is it a great way to give back, but it also brings passion and purpose to their own lives.

"Working on behalf of companion animals is so important," Bernadette Peters said. "We start to realize how healing they are."

My neighbor Gloria, who is semi-retired, fosters dogs. The dogs are lucky to have her, but she's lucky, too, because they keep her connected to everyone and everything in the neighborhood. Rain or shine, she's always out walking them, and the dogs know which driveways to drag her into for a quick conversation.

My friend Pam Kramer has been rescuing animals for over 30 years. She also helps keep dogs and cats alive by telling their stories via social networking and at www.examiner.com/pets-in-chicago/pamela-kramer. Taking a moment to share one of her articles or posts might well save an animal's life.

I love animals. Over the years, I've signed almost as many copies of the *Must Love Dogs* series to readers' dogs and cats as I have to readers. My family and I have always adopted shelter animals, which I personally believe make the best pets, maybe because they're so grateful to get a second chance.

And still, when our beloved dog Daisy died at 15, Jake and I decided we'd be pet-free. We'd spent most of our years together nurturing kids and animals, and now we wanted to focus on us. To be footloose and fancy free like we were when we were first dating. We didn't want the hassle of finding a pet sitter. We didn't want to worry about our pets while we traveled. Most of all, I think, we didn't want our hearts to be broken again by another animal who would die on us someday.

I tell the whole story in *Never Too Late*, but we had exactly one footloose and fancy-free weeklong trip. And when we got back, we found out that a feral cat had given birth to four kittens under our front porch.

Hawks were circling, we spotted a coyote, the temperature was dropping fast. So we staged a high drama rescue. We saved them all. And we kept them.

When I look at the first photos of those four tiny, dirt-covered kittens and their terrified mother, who was barely more than a kitten herself, it always makes my eyes tear up. No matter how many mistakes we make from here on out, no matter how we screw up, my family and I will always know that we saved five lives.

Our rescue cats have turned our entire lives upside down. They've knocked fragile things off shelves, chewed the pulls off custom blinds, wreaked havoc on my daily pages by walking across the computer keyboard as I type. Between them, they have black, white and orange fur in various combinations, which means that no matter what you wear, one color of shedding cat hair will show up on it. And yet these cats are high up on the list of the best things that have ever happened to us.

Two of the now-grown kittens have gone up the street to live with our daughter and son-in-law. Every morning the other three wake me by jumping up on the bed, licking my arms, kneading my back, head-butting me. Pebbles, the formerly feral mama cat, who everyone said would never adjust to inside life, is often the first one up on the bed. Sunshine purrs like a muffled motorboat. Squiggy always falls off the bed at least once.

The experts say that just asking ourselves what we're

grateful for can make us happier. Lots of people keep gratitude journals, and I think that's another great use for your Shine On notebook. Writing down the things we're grateful for every day can have a big positive impact on our mental as well as our physical health.

But I think of my cats as a living gratitude journal. While they crawl all over me, I start every day by making a mental list of the things I'm grateful for, beginning with how lucky I am that these fabulous felines came into my life. Not a day goes by that they don't make me laugh. Their sweetness and gentleness and their ability to enjoy the moment—the squirrel outside the window, the drip of the bathtub faucet, the unparalleled thrill of fresh kitty litter—inspire me every day.

"There has never been a cat/Who couldn't calm me down/By walking slowly/Past my chair," Rod McKuen wrote.

Studies have shown that there are massive emotional, physical, and mental benefits to spending time with pets. Pets provide companionship, as well as unconditional love and acceptance. Stroking our pets lowers our blood pressure and our stress levels. Playing with them releases endorphins, those feel-good chemicals in our brain, making us feel calmer, more relaxed, happier.

Pet owners recover from illnesses faster than people who don't own pets. Pets ease our loneliness, give us a reason to live, a purpose in life. Walking a dog is great exercise, as is running down the hallway dragging a feathery cat wand.

"Animals are such agreeable friends—they ask no questions; they pass no criticisms," George Eliot wrote.

I can't think of a more awesome thing to aspire to as the years go by than becoming a crazy cat lady. Or a demented dog lady.

I've also learned that owning multiple animals is actually easier than owning one, since they have one another for company. So rescue if you can. Adopt. Foster. Volunteer. Cat-sit. Start a dog walking business like three boomer women do in *Must Love Dogs: Bark & Roll Forever.*

I even know of a couple that has turned their house into a sanctuary for rabbits. The rabbits are all litter box trained, but rabbits are chewers by nature, so making the house rabbit friendly included some serious rewiring as well as the installation of indestructible metal wainscoting on the walls. But this couple says it's impossible to feel stressed in a house full of rabbits, and opening their home to them has filled their lives with joy.

To Botox or Not To Botox

The conference I'm speaking at is filled with awesome women. Maureen is reinventing her life after a divorce. Karen has just become an empty nester. Carol is trying to decide whether or not to move. Barbara is working on a novel. Lisa is a professional organizer. I love chatting with them all as I sign their books—listening to their stories feeds me not only as a writer, but as a person.

And they're the perfect group to speak to about reinvention. In my head The Beatles break into "Sergeant Pepper's Lonely Hearts Club Band." They're such a lovely audience, I really would love to take them home with me.

One of the perks of the conference is that I get to listen to the other speakers. A dietician talks about the latest eating trends and makes me feel good about my new sugar and grain-free lifestyle. A financial advisor tells us how to get smarter about money. A book guru (Yay, Robin of Reading with Robin!) fills us in on the benefits of joining a book club.

A physician talks about women's sexual health. Addyi, the "female Viagra," is just about to come out, and he gets a huge laugh when he tells us that it didn't do so well in the clinical trials on post-menopausal women because "they're more strong-willed and tend to know what they do and don't want." He's brought samples of Überlube, a paraben and preservative-free sexual lubricant that he seems to be a bit more optimistic about.

"Coconut oil is supposed to be a great lubricant," a woman behind me says.

Of course it is.

A dermatologist is up next. As he discusses the importance of wearing sunscreen and staying out of the sun, I'm nodding along with the rest of the audience. But I have to admit I'm also trying to figure out how he got that George Hamilton tan of his if he stays out of the sun. Self-tanner? Airbrush makeup?

Growing up before the sunscreen era, my sisters and I used to get lobster-red sunburns and then take turns peeling long strips of dead skin off one another's backs a few days later. In high school, my friends and I doused ourselves in baby oil, then covered double record album covers with aluminum foil and positioned them under our faces to make sure we caught every single ray of sun.

Like most of us, I've been religious about using sunscreen for decades now. Neutrogena Ultra Sheer Liquid is one of my favorites, as are Kiss My Face and Blue Lizard, which are both made with titanium dioxide and zinc oxide instead of chemicals that sting my sensitive eyes. I also slather on moisturizer—some of my faves are Cerave, Olay Regenerist, my new best friend coconut oil.

The dermatologist clicks his remote. PowerPoint slides of midlife women's faces fill two huge screens on either side of the podium. Wrinkled faces. Non-wrinkled faces. Faces filled with personality. Faces filled with fillers.

"I wish I had a twin so I could know what I'd look like without plastic surgery," Joan Rivers used to joke.

As the dermatologist does his thing, I'm thinking that it's

hard to sit through a pitch like this without wondering what we'd look like with a little bit of this or a little bit of that.

Some women I know get Botox, but pretend they don't. Others are open about using injectables, but draw the line at plastic surgery. I have a Facebook friend I've never met who posts photos of her cream-covered face from her dermatologist's office: *Getting ready for Botox and fillers. Stay tuned for after pics!*

I haven't done any of it, and I have absolutely no intention of jumping onboard. I know this isn't the path to shining on for me. I can think of a gazillion better ways to spend my time and money. For me, a far more effective strategy than Botox is to embrace who I am and stop looking over my shoulder to compare myself to everybody else.

Personally, I don't even think these procedures make us look better. I think they can make our faces look glassy and fake, and eventually, kind of heartbreaking. Give me warmth and expression, crinkly foreheads and crow's feet, any day—they're all signs of a life well lived.

"I've had a little plastic surgery," Jamie Lee Curtis has said. "I've had a little lipo. I've had a little Botox. And you know what? None of it works. None of it."

"I think your whole life shows in your face and you should be proud of that," Lauren Bacall said.

I agree. But I also know that lots of women feel differently. It's our money and our time and our face, so bottom line, if you think this stuff will help you shine on, go for it.

Me, I just pick up a free sample of Überlube on the way out.

Tapping

I have a great time at the conference. I meet lots of fabulous women, and I even manage to fit in two long rejuvenating walks along the ocean. I eat well, too, finding plenty of choices on restaurant menus and asking the waitperson to substitute a side salad for anything I'm no longer eating.

On the plane ride to my next stop, I take one more look at the answers to my Facebook question about trying new things. Cheryl says she would try ballroom dancing. Sandra wants to try ballroom dance, too. Brandy is obsessed with *Dancing with the Stars* and would love to learn from the pro dancers. Myrtle also wants to learn to ballroom dance. Denise says she would try ballroom dance and learn to play the piano, though not at the same time. Phyllis says she would learn to dance ballroom style.

Jocelyn would dance. And wonderful book advocate that she is, she reminds me that I've already written about this world. In *Wallflower in Bloom*, my novel about a midlife personal assistant to her famous brother who uses his massive online following to get herself voted on as a last-minute replacement on *Dancing with the Stars*.

I had such a blast researching that novel, learning everything I could about ballroom dancing, following the blogs and posts of the show's pro and celebrity dancers, as well as of the costume designers and makeup artists. I shadowed ballroom dance teachers, watched competitions, sat in on classes. I immersed myself in the world of ballroom dance, danced every step of every dance scene in my head as I wrote it.

"Dance is a vertical expression of a horizontal desire," Robert Frost said. George Bernard Shaw seconded the sentiment, though he changed vertical to perpendicular.

"The body says what words cannot," Martha Graham said.

Perhaps this quote from *Wallflower in Bloom* is a better fit for my own personal ballroom dance experience: "To dance is to live, if you live through the dance."

Jake and I took ballroom dancing lessons together back when our kids were little. Let's just say it wasn't our finest eight weeks together. We were both exhausted by the end of the day. We worried about leaving the kids with a babysitter. Jake accused me of trying to lead. I said somebody had to.

When I was growing up, I took lots of dance classes, from ballet to jazz to Irish step. I went on to take belly-dancing classes in college, to teach dance aerobics after college. Whenever I get the chance, I take a Zumba class. I have no noticeable talent, but I've always loved dance of all kinds, and maybe most of all those *Big Chill* moments when you put on some classic rock and just dance around the kitchen.

I go back to the Facebook posts. Beth would learn to tap dance. Up until I read her words, I've completely forgotten the tap dancing lessons I took as an adult. I can no longer recall whether it was a few years before or a few years after the ballroom dance lessons, but I remember how much fun it was. And how surprisingly challenging, though I'm proud to say that I eventually managed to learn how to shuffle off to Buffalo (full disclosure: in one direction only).

Tap dancing is all about using your footwork, and the

metal plates attached to the bottom of your tap shoes, to create different sounds and rhythms. It's almost like a mathematical equation or even a conversation—as if your feet are talking to the music and to each other.

Wow, I realize, it's exactly like drumming. But with your feet.

I can't wait to find out if I still have my tap shoes.

So once I'm home again, I get a good night's sleep and finish writing my daily pages. Then I go on a hunt for my tap shoes. Just when I'm starting to think I must have thrown them out decades ago, I find them—ribbon-tied, black patent leather Capezios—in a box out in the garage that hasn't been unpacked yet even though we've been here for a few years now.

I'm psyched. I carry my tap shoes into my office. When I find out they still fit, I'm double psyched.

I wake up my computer to track down a tap class. When I Google *adult tap*, the first thing that pops up is a bar. It's a bit early in the morning for tap dancing on bar tops, so I keep scrolling.

It turns out there are a couple of adult tap dance classes within driving distance. As I contemplate signing up for one, I flash back to attending one of my old friend Maribara's adult dance recitals and remember how she and the rest of the costumed dancing midlife women were in their glory. There's also a group of midlife women at my gym who have organized themselves into a group called The Kickers. I've peeked through the window at their rehearsals, and what they do looks like a cross between a dance number in a Broadway musical and a drill team performance at half time.

I know these women are having a blast. Practices and performances give them camaraderie as well as accountability. But I realize I don't want to schedule anything, to make this a group thing. And I definitely don't want to perform. I just want to play with my tap shoes.

So I pull up a YouTube beginner tap tutorial on my iPad and dance along with it. *Brush front. Brush side. Ball change. Step ball change. Kick ball change. Flap brush step*. I move on to *heel toe-toe heel-heel toe-toe heel.* I pause the video and repeat that last group of steps faster and faster until I think it might almost look like I have half a clue what I'm doing.

I can only imagine what the UPS guy would think if he saw me through the window, but I'm having too much fun to care. Maybe I can get away with wearing my tap shoes to the next drumming circle at the park.

My cats are sitting in a row watching me, completely mesmerized. I make exaggerated jazz hand circles and tap the length of the hallway and back for them. All three cats turn their heads in perfect synch to follow me.

Maybe I can teach them to tap dance. To "Alley Cat," of course. I could even make a video, which I have no doubt would so go viral.

I take a quick break to Google up how to teach cats to tap dance. All I come up with is a mom blog tutorial on how to turn any shoes into tap shoes with baby food jar tops. I have a flash of pure, unadulterated midlife joy that my own baby food days are behind me.

Instead, I've become a crazy cat lady. Not only a crazy cat lady, but a crazy tap dancing cat lady.

Awesome sauce.

And Tapping

"Fear is a fact of a well-lived life," I say in *Never Too Late*. I also talk about both fear of success and fear of failure in that book. That even though success can be terrifying, when it happens we find a way to handle it. That fear of failure requires pushing past our perfectionism. When we allow ourselves to try things and fail, we realize that every failure is an opportunity to figure out how to do it better the next time. Bottom line, pushing past the fear is how we get to all the good places.

And then there's the other kind of fear, the physical kind that can turn into a phobia: heights, germs, crowds, etc. I've learned how important it is to face these fears if we're going to grow awesome instead of old. Otherwise, we start to restructure our lives to avoid the things we're afraid of. The more we avoid them, the more power they take on. And the more our world shrinks.

During my tap dance Googling stint, I stumble on another variety of tapping altogether. This kind of tapping is also called EFT, or Emotional Freedom Technique, as well as TFT, or Thought Field Therapy. It's a kind of self-soothing that's reputed to be particularly effective with anxiety. I've seen it described as a combination of Chinese acupressure and modern psychology.

I'm fascinated so I read some more about it. And tapping seems pretty accessible. When you're feeling anxious or afraid, you just use the fingertips on one or both hands to gently tap some of your body's meridian accupoints—the top of your head, your eyebrows, the outside edge of your eye sockets, under your eyes, under your nose, midway between the bottom of your lip and your chin, under your collarbones, under your arms, the web between your thumbs and pointer fingers, the karate chop spot on the outside of your hands—tapping 5 to 7 times on each point. It's supposed to calm you down and also make your fear and anxiety more manageable.

Some of the women I know are afraid of things like snakes and spiders and basements and elevators. Quite a few of them are terrified of flying. High up on my own personal fear list is highway driving. When I gave this fear to Melanie in my novel *Time Flies*, I found out how common it is. Since that book came out, so many women have told me that highway driving terrifies them, too.

I have to admit I've been guilty of trying to maneuver my life so I don't have to drive very often or very far. I know how self-limiting this is, and in my quest to shine on, I've been working on it.

I've come to realize that disaster fantasizing about what might happen is what feeds my highway anxiety. *Oh, no*, that hotshot who's driving too fast is going to hit me when he cuts me off. *Yikes*, I'll never get over to the next lane, which means I won't make my exit and I'll spend the rest of my life trapped on this highway.

The fact that awful things have probably happened to us by this point in our lives, like the huge piece of scrap metal that once flew off the truck in front of the car I was riding in and shattered our windshield while we were driving, doesn't help this kind of thinking.

I try to reframe my thoughts. I tell myself I'm safe and that whatever happens, I'll handle it. I tell myself that I'm in charge, not the fear. That the more I make myself drive, the easier it will get. That even if it takes me a while to conquer this, even if I fail sometimes, I'm getting closer. If I hang in, eventually I'll get there.

But anxiety is a grind. Our hearts beat faster. We can experience rapid breathing, trembling, numbness or tingling in the hands, stomach pains, dizziness. It's no fun.

So I figure a little tapping couldn't hurt.

I choose a Sunday morning when almost everybody will either be sleeping in or getting dressed for church. I map out a highway route that I would normally circumvent by checking Avoid Highways on my GPS and weaving my way through the back roads.

Just thinking about doing this causes my anxiety level to ramp up, so I start tapping in my driveway. I feel beyond foolish as I tap my way down from head to hands, but I have to admit it's pretty calming.

Though I also have to admit I haven't even left my driveway yet.

Hardly anyone's on the road, so I tap again at each red light I come to on the way to the entrance ramp. And when I hit the highway, I really think all that tapping has helped. It's not like I'm cured—I still totally hate highway driving—but my anxiety level is maybe half what it usually is.

For me, tapping turns out to be a simple, useful strategy to add to my bag of tricks. I use it not just when anxiety kicks in, but when I'm struggling with my daily pages or I can't fall asleep. I've done so much speaking by now that it doesn't make me nervous very often anymore, but tapping is a great way to clear my head and get focused before I speak.

And while tapping isn't something I'd ever do in public, it doesn't take a lot of space either. So it's another great use for the privacy of a restroom stall!

Photophobia

Photobombing is the act of unexpectedly appearing in a photo—accidentally, purposely, or accidentally on purpose. It's often done as a practical joke. People at weddings do it. Tourists do it. Statues do it. Fans do it. Celebrities do it. Animals do it, perhaps best of all.

In fact, and I just scrolled through about a dozen photobombing sites to make sure, pretty much the only animate or inanimate things you can count on not to photobomb are midlife women. When a camera appears, a prank is usually the furthest thing from most of our minds.

Because we're too busy hiding.

If we have time, we scurry to the bathroom and hope nobody misses us. If we can't escape altogether, we use a small child, a large dog, a tree, or a tall-backed upholstered chair for a body block. In a group shot, we dive behind two broad-shouldered people in the back row.

When I flip through my own family photos, there are tons of my two kids, quite a few of my husband, and almost none of me. Because in the most brilliant photophobic ploy of all, I became the one who took the photos so I didn't have to be in them.

How we feel about having our picture taken is often tied to our overall self-esteem. Not liking the way we look in photographs is one more way of not liking ourselves, one more way of feeling less than. Facing our photophobia can help us shine on.

I'm not sure I ever would have faced my own fear of the camera if I hadn't been forced to when my first book was published when I was 45. Suddenly I needed an author photo. Readers wanted pictures with me when I signed their books at events. Newspapers and magazines sent photographers, and not only would they notice if I hid in the bathroom, but I was pretty sure I couldn't talk them into taking a picture of one of my cute kids or pets instead.

When my novel *Must Love Dogs* was made into a movie when I was 50, giving in to my photophobia was not an option. As I walked the red carpet at the Hollywood premiere, I did 35 interviews, most of them including popping flashes or rolling cameras. It was scary, but also a huge opportunity to get the word out about my books.

Over the course of my midlife author gig, I've made tons of mistakes and there are plenty of cringe worthy photos of me out there to prove it. But I've also learned some cool stuff that has upped my chances of getting a good photograph, things that might help you when you decide to face your own photophobia. (Or the next time you can't manage to hide from a camera!)

First of all, whoever said the camera doesn't lie was a total liar. Of course it lies. A photograph isn't the recording of fact. It's the split-second capturing of a single angle, and often not our best one. Especially if we're looking at the camera like it's the enemy.

So if the camera is going to lie anyway, the trick is to get it to lie in our favor. The more we can step out of victim mode and help the photo along, the happier we're going to be with the results.

It also helps to remember that when we look at this photo 20 years from now, we'll think we looked pretty damn good, if we do say so ourselves. Just the way when we look at that picture of us standing on the beach in that barely-there bathing suit 20 or 30 or 40 years ago, we wish we'd been able to appreciate how hot we looked back then. It's hard to see our own beauty except in hindsight.

The first thing I figured out was that, even if I wasn't crazy about the way I looked, I'd rather see a photo of me smiling than one of me looking terrified or shut down. The camera can't capture our sparkling personality if we're not showing it. So don't just stand there—work it a little. Laugh, make a joke, forget about how much you hate having your picture taken and think about fun stuff. Give the camera something awesome to capture.

I learned the hard way how important a flattering angle can be when a rookie photographer squatted down and shot up at me for a photo to accompany an article. I think he was going for powerful, but the result was a pretty horrifying combination of nostrils, chins, and jowls.

When the person taking the picture points the camera down on you by holding the camera slightly higher than your head, the resulting photo is almost always more flattering, especially at midlife. Once I caught on to this angle advantage, I used to joke that I was going to rent a crane for my next author photo. And then I started seeing photos online that had been taken from this extreme vantage point, and it looked as if these women were gazing into the heavens at some kind of miraculous religious vision. So be careful not to overdo it, unless the I've-just-seen-God look is what you're going for!

A more experienced photographer taught me a trick during a big charity event. As I was lining up with the other speakers for a group shot, two well-known female authors both dove for the middle, elbowing me out of the way from either side. Hard, as in I had bruises to show for it.

I mean, what was I going to do, pull their hair? So I just found another place at one end of the line.

The photographer saw the whole thing and walked me back to the middle of the line. After the photo, he approached me again. "The people in the center of a group shot always look better," he said. "Don't let them push you around."

I still don't think the best spot is worth elbowing anyone for, but it's good to know that fighting our urge to hide on the sidelines will make for a better photograph.

When we're photophobic, it shows in our body language. We have a tendency to hunch over to try to make ourselves disappear, so it's important to remember that standing up straight with our shoulders back makes us look better in photographs. As does extending our neck to make it as long as possible and lifting our chin slightly.

Experimenting with different angles helps, too. Try turning your body at a 45-degree angle and then twisting your head toward the camera. Try tilting your head. Or turn your head slightly to the right or left, which can give your features more dimension.

For a long time, I never knew quite what to do with my arms during photos, so I just let them kind of hang there dangling. And then I learned that putting one or both hands on my hips—casually, as opposed to like a cheerleader—not only gave me attitude, but much better lines.

Good lighting is key, too. Think soft, soft, soft. Light coming in from a window. A street light shining on our face. A scarf draped over a lampshade.

There are two times of day when the natural light is so flattering it makes everybody look better. One is just after dawn. Unfortunately, like many midlife women, my face doesn't wake up until a couple hours after I do, so this doesn't work for me.

My perfect light is at dusk, just as the sun is beginning to set. Try it—it's magical.

Maybe the biggest thing I learn is that to a large degree a good photograph is a numbers game. One and done usually doesn't cut it when it comes to getting a great photo. But if someone takes, say, 25 gazillion photos of me, I'm almost guaranteed to think I look okay in one of them.

Take a Picture, It Lasts Longer

If you think a decent photo of yourself is like a unicorn—you know, a mythical creature that you're pretty sure doesn't really exist—then going after that one fabulous photo can be really empowering.

Of course there are more important things in life than how we look in photos. But the digital age has changed everything. The moment we go on Facebook, which is where all the midlife women are hanging out these days, we have an online presence.

Also, everywhere we look we're bombarded with heavily Photoshopped images of celebrities. These women don't really look like this, but it's hard to remember that. And it's easy to start to feel bad about the way we look.

Obviously, if the quest for your unicorn photo feels like the ultimate in vanity to you, don't do it. But if you're still using the blue silhouette default avatar, or your high school graduation photo, or a picture of a sunflower from your garden as your Facebook profile picture, maybe it's time. Or maybe you've started a midlife blog and need a photo of yourself for the About Me section.

A woman in one of my reinvention workshops, a cancer survivor, told us that she used to wake up in the middle of the night worrying about which crappy photo would run with her obituary if she didn't make it. At the first break, all the budding photographers in the group whipped out their phones for an impromptu photo session. She got some great shots.

A selfie is one way to go, although it's hard to get a good selfie. The limited length of our arm results in holding the camera too close to our face, which has a flattening effect on our features, not usually our best look. That extended arm in the photo is also a dead giveaway, so if you do go that route, don't pretend it's not a selfie!

A selfie stick can up the odds of getting a good selfie, since it can stretch longer than your arm can. It feels like less of a narcissistic cliché if you think of it as a tripod, which is essentially what it is. A selfie stick comes in handy when you're traveling, too, since it allows you to photograph yourself standing in front of all sorts of cool things. Selfie sticks have come way down in price (just search Amazon for the ones with the best prices and reviews). If you buy one with Bluetooth, you won't have to worry about getting a blurry photo when you push the button on the kind connected by actual cord to the camera.

Glamour shots were big back in the '80s and '90s, and if feather boas and your hair blowing in the wind machine sound fun to you, go for it. There are still plenty of photographers out there taking photos like that. You can track one down, maybe even invite some like-minded friends over and turn it into a feather boa photo party.

I prefer more casual photos, which I think look hipper and more alive than formal shots, glamour or otherwise. You can treat yourself to a session with a photographer who does casual outdoor portraits. Or find a friend who needs a good photo, too, and take turns shooting until you both get at least one photo you like.

What I've started doing is this: When I'm dressed to go out and wearing actual makeup and everything, instead of hiding from the camera, I ask my husband or one of my kids to take a few photos. Every once in a while I get a good one that I can use for my website or even as an author photo for one of my books, especially with a little bit of photo editing.

As for photo editing, I used to joke that Photoshop is the creative woman's Botox. But then an author I know had a really glam, heavily Photoshopped author photo done. When she went off on book tour, nobody recognized her. And at every stop along the way, at least one person gave her a puzzled look and said, *You looked so beautiful in that picture on your book cover.*

I don't want people to be disappointed when they meet me in the flesh. I want them to recognize me. Once I even politely asked someone I'd hired to take an author photo for the original files so I could get my crow's feet back. She'd Photoshopped them right out. Not only did I look so, so fake, but my personality had vanished along with my wrinkles.

Which doesn't mean that I think a little bit of creative photo editing is a bad thing. If we don't like our upper arms, we can get rid of those suckers by cropping them right out and making the photo more of a close-up. Ditto for our hips or our abdomen. I was recently scrolling through my feed and stopped at a new profile picture a Facebook friend I've never met had just posted. It was a great candid shot loaded with personality—as well as a big blob of salad dressing on her T-shirt, just above her left breast. We've all done it, but it's definitely a crop-able moment.

Chances are your camera, and even the camera on your phone, have photo-editing capabilities built right in. Google up a tutorial or play around until you figure out how to use them. Email yourself the original photo first, so you have a backup.

I'm a huge fan of Photoshop Elements, a simplified

version of Photoshop, and as an author/publisher I use it all the time, both as a photo editor and to create lots of fun stuff. But there are plenty of photo editors out there that are free and also allow you to work online instead of installing another program on your computer.

As I was researching them to find a good one to suggest, I was thrilled to learn that Adobe now offers a free, web-based basic photo editor called Photoshop Express, which you can access from any computer connected to the Internet.

It took me a while to find it, so here's the direct link: http://www.photoshop.com/tools?wf=editor. Once you get there, you might want to bookmark the page so you can find it again. Then look down past the sales pitch until you see Photoshop Express Editor. Click on Start the Editor. Then click on Upload a Photo. Click on Upload and choose a photo from your computer. Click on Touchup and place the cursor over that glob of salad dressing on your T-shirt to get rid of it. Crop the photo to turn it into a close-up. Play around with different effects by trying some of the other tools—just hit Undo if you do something you don't like. When you're finished, click Done in the lower right hand corner. When asked what you'd like to do with your edited photo, click Save to my Computer. Then you'll be asked where to save it. I usually save it to my desktop so I can find it easily.

Another helpful online tool to know about is Canva.com. If you want to create a cool Facebook cover photo—the larger area behind your profile pic—just click on the Facebook Cover Photo template. Upload one of your own photos, or choose a free background, or you can upload a premium background for a dollar. Add some text if you'd like, maybe a quote that inspires you. When you're finished, just click Download at the top of the screen. Easy breezy. You can also design everything from blog post graphics to invitations to flyers on Canva.

Not long ago: Jake and I are staying at the beach for a

wedding. Mostly I'm looking forward to taking a break and having some fun. But because we don't live near the beach right now, I've also got one goal—to get at least one decent candid photo on the beach for my beachy books.

The thing about that perfect light is that it sneaks up on you. The sun is too harsh and too bright, but then suddenly, abracadabra, that magical light is here. So I'm trying not to sweat off my makeup as I tell Jake to just keep taking pictures. And because he's very precise and meticulous, the kind of guy who would line up one shot perfectly while I took 50, by the time he takes a picture, I've been holding still for what feels like forever, and the look in my eyes says, *Will you hurry up already?*

So I'm getting testy and Jake's getting testy, in that dance that every long-term couple knows. And in the middle of all this, a perfect stranger walks up and asks us if we want him to take our picture.

I've heard the horror stories, too, and I suppose he could have run off with the camera, but you've got to trust your instincts. And besides, it's not that valuable a camera.

So Jake hands him the camera and he takes a couple photos of us, just as the perfect light arrives. And then he and Jake start to chat. And I'm trying to think of how we can get rid of this guy without being rude before we lose the light. So finally I just blurt out that I'm an author, and excuse us for just a minute, but we really need to get some photos on the beach.

And it turns out his name is Stuart Wilson and he's a photographer. He doesn't have a camera with him, but between my camera and a surprisingly good camera on his phone, he gets me the photos I was hoping for, and more—he's really talented. Then we start chatting, and he tells us that he's just retired from his corporate job and has been thinking about doing more photography, something he's always done on the side.

So I encourage him. And he lets me use the photos. And Jake is off the hook. Happy ending all around.

Since that serendipitous encounter, I always offer to take photos for strangers. So if our paths cross and you think of it first, don't hesitate to ask!

Fighting Your Inner Dinosaur Some More

Maybe you skimmed right over those last sections since you have absolutely no need for a profile photo. Because you don't do Facebook, or any other kind of social networking. Ever. End of story.

It's your life, of course, but the digital age is here, and if you let yourself be left behind, you'll be a dinosaur before you know it. Statistics show that the majority of midlife women are on Facebook right now. So it's as simple as this: If you're not, you're missing the party!

Social networking, when used well, enhances our personal relationships. It's such a fun and easy way to reconnect with old friends and make new ones, as well to maintain our existing relationships. It challenges our brains with learning new skills—as long as we don't spend all our time watching cute pet videos! Social networking helps us avoid isolation. It helps us stay current. Facebook birthdays are the best—all those happy wishes lined up one after another can be incredibly uplifting.

I've reconnected with so many people and made lots of new friends on Facebook, which has definitely enriched my life. And while Facebook is the place where most midlife women are hanging out online right now, there are lots of other social networking options, too. If you have a passion for cooking, design, fashion, crafts, and pretty much anything that's visually appealing, Pinterest is a terrific option for you. Instagram is a great place to post the photos you take, which can become a kind of photo diary. I wasn't a big fan of Twitter at first, but I gave it a try anyway, and I've met lots of interesting people there.

Some women tell me they can't figure out Facebook because they're luddites. They're technophobes. They're just not good at computers. Getting our tech together is a huge part of shining on. There's always a learning curve, but the sooner we push ourselves beyond it, the sooner we'll have the skills we need and the better we'll feel. Ask a friend or family member to be your computer mentor and help you get up to speed. Google up some tutorials. Take a class at your local library or a continuing education program.

Other midlife women tell me that they shy away from social networking because they don't want everyone to know their personal business. Easy enough: just don't post anything you don't want people to know. You can also adjust your privacy settings and divide your Facebook friends into lists to further control who sees what you share. You can even join or create private Facebook groups—I'm in a few, including one for midlife reinventors (go to Facebook.com/groups/NeverTooLateReinvention and click Join Group if you'd like to join us!), several for writers, one for my family, and one for my high school graduating class. Unless you're a member of the group, you can't see our posts.

So don't let social networking pass you by. Give it a real chance. Embrace it as one more way to grow awesome instead of old.

Barefootin'

Robert Parker jumps out of 1965 to sing "Barefootin'" to me as I walk along the beach. Walking barefoot on the sand is one of the best things about being at the beach for a long weekend, and I'm enjoying every moment of it. It's like getting a foot massage and a workout at the same time.

I learned a lot about the benefits of beach walking when I researched my novel *The Wildwater Walking Club*. When we walk barefoot, we stimulate important reflexology points and nerve endings on the soles of our feet. Because the sand provides resistance, beach walking is more difficult than walking on hard surfaces. When our feet sink into the sand, the muscles in our feet and legs have to work harder. Walking on the changing surface of the beach helps improve our agility and balance, too, and like all walking, it improves our circulation.

Feeling the sand between our toes intensifies our sensory experience and helps us stay in the moment. We notice the cry of the gulls. The crash of the waves. The salty bite of the air. The dried seaweed and shell bits we step over at the high tide line. The hermit crab that scuttles across the sand carrying its shell house on its back. The piece of sea glass sparkling up at us like a treasure.

As kids growing up in a beach town, my friends and I used to have contests to see who could go barefoot from the moment summer vacation began until school started up again in the fall. All summer long hot tar burned callouses, thick and leathery, onto the bottoms of our feet. We'd sneak right by the No Bare Feet Allowed signs at the entrance to the ice cream parlor or the movie theater. Our hot feet practically sizzled when we waded into the cold ocean.

I still hate wearing shoes. One of the first things I do when I walk into my house is take them off. Since I work at home, I spend the vast majority of my time barefoot. We even have a beach pebble tile floor in our master bathroom shower, which might be a bit bumpy for some people, but to me it's the ultimate in foot pampering.

A woman I met at the garden center created a reflexology garden path out of river rocks. She kicks off her shoes and strolls the path barefoot so she gets a foot massage while she visits her garden.

I have a rocking footrest with massage balls on it under my desk, a gift I received years ago that I still use all the time. Although I have to admit that since I've started sitting on my purple exercise ball to write, I'm careful to take turns with them since using them both at once seems like a recipe for disaster.

My maternal grandmother was one of nine children and wore hand-me-down shoes throughout her childhood. I can still vividly remember that she put cotton balls between her misshapen toes to ease the pain and made weekly visits to the podiatrist. My paternal grandmother was a nurse, and the moment she got home from the 3 to 11 shift, she'd mix a drink, turn on *The Johnny Carson Show*, take off her white nurse's shoes, sink into a chair, and put her aching feet up on the ottoman.

Many of our foot problems, including bunions, corns, calluses, blisters, ingrown toenails, and toenail fungus, are caused or aggravated by wearing shoes. High-heeled shoes are the biggest culprits of them all, deforming our feet and throwing off our posture, which can cause knee, hip, ankle, and back pain along with the obvious squished-toe pain.

So giving our feet some breathing time seems like a good idea. Barefoot advocates say that our feet can even become stronger and more flexible when we ditch the shoes as much as possible.

Strong feet can significantly reduce our risk of falling. Simple things like lifting our toes while keeping our heels on the ground, making the shape of a W as we tap our toes up and down, can help strengthen our feet. We can stand with our toes on the edge of a stair step, hang onto the railing, and drop our heels below the edge of the step. We can walk a barefoot loop around our house on our tippy-toes, then walk another loop on our heels.

You can Google up lots of good foot exercises. My favorite, because I can really feel it working my plantar fascia, which connects the heel to the front of the foot and supports the arch along the way, is to roll out a towel and dump a bunch of marbles on it. Then you pick up the marbles one-by-one with your toes and drop them into a coffee mug or a jar. Start doing this while you're sitting and then work up to standing (with a wall nearby in case you need to grab it), which will also improve your balance. It's challenging. My cats love it, too, and they keep batting the marbles all over the house, which makes it even more challenging!

As I research this section, there's an old idea called earthing or grounding that has apparently circled around again and keeps popping up. The theory goes that positive electrons in the form of free radicals build up in our bodies, and when we come into direct contact with the earth by walking barefoot on it or sitting on it, we pick up the earth's negative electrons, which balances out our electric energy level. Still with me? Anyway, this is supposed to help improve our sleep, reduce pain and chronic inflammation, lower our stress levels.

I'm certainly not an expert so I have no idea if there's something to this earthing stuff or if it's just full-blown batsh*t crazy. But who knows, maybe that's why I like walking barefoot on the beach so much.

Any excuse to head outside barefoot and stand on the tickle of green grass and the warm mulch of a garden bed seems like a good thing to me. So as soon as I get home from the beach, that's exactly what I do.

Weigh In

"Wow, you look great! How much weight have you lost?" people post when photos from a conference show up online.

"Thanks so much!" I answer, side-stepping the question. But it reminds me that I actually have no idea how much weight I've lost. So the next morning, before I even put on my writing pajamas, I step on the scale for the first time in forever.

I don't know quite what to make of the number on the scale. It's a respectable number, but it's also surprisingly meaningless. My life is no more and no less perfect than it was when I avoided weighing myself because I didn't want to face a bigger number.

What I know is that I'm so over the diet mentality.

"As it turns out," Carrie Fisher said, "I really like being congratulated on my weight loss. I like it so much, it's tragic."

I get that. I think most of us have been there. As lovely as it is to receive compliments and as much as I appreciate them, that's the trap I never want to fall into again. I don't want to need other people to validate my weight loss so I can feel good about myself.

"I'm prouder of my weight loss than my Oscar," Jennifer Hudson once said.

I'm a gazillion times prouder of my work and my family, both two and four-legged, than I am of my own weight loss. To be fair, even if Jennifer Hudson meant what she said at the time, I bet she is, too.

By midlife we all know there's a massive emotional component to the weight thing. I don't at all believe we need to be thin, or thinner, to shine on. I think we should rock what we've got, but I also know that we have to feel good in our own skin in order to do that.

I'm happy. I'm healthy. I want to live my life, not obsess about my weight.

I also feel really good eating this way. And just in case you're looking for something to eat, here's one of my favorite salads:

Shine On Go-To Salad

1 cooked boneless chicken breast, chopped into
bite-size pieces (or a few slices of nitrate-free turkey or a
handful of cooked shrimp)
4 cups Romaine lettuce, chopped
1 oz. cheese, your choice, shredded or broken into small pieces
½ avocado, chopped
handful broccoli florets
handful organic grape tomatoes, halved
slice red onion, chopped
a slice or two cooked bacon, chopped
handful sunflower seeds
pink Himalayan salt and pepper to taste

Just throw it all together and drizzle with apple cider vinegar (or lemon juice) and olive oil. Or use your favorite salad dressing.

Winter, Spring, Summer or Fall

As I finish my morning walk and roll my purple exercise ball into place again, Carole King is singing "You've Got a Friend."

I first discovered which colors were my friends back in the early '80s when we were all getting our colors done. With my dark brown hair, deep hazel eyes, and fair skin with cool blue undertones, I was a Clear Winter. Primary colors and cool icy colors worked best on me. I could up my chances of getting a compliment by wearing red.

Because I think it might be fun, after I finish my daily pages I start cruising the Internet to brush up on seasonal color theory. Apparently I'm still a Winter, but my gray hair has moved me from the Clear Winter to the Cool Winter category. The colors that work for me now are slightly lighter—essentially, they have more white in them—but they still need to be bold enough that I don't look washed out. Warm yellowy colors have never looked that great on me, but now they're the enemy, along with golden browns and oranges.

I've already figured out that blue—from icy to cobalt to cornflower to periwinkle—is now the color mostly likely to generate compliments. Some of the color experts say that charcoal gray and navy will look better on me now than black. Others say black and pure winter white is a great combo for me. I know I'll never give up black, so I'll just brighten it up with accessories if I need to. Silver jewelry will trump gold by a long shot on me, especially if it sparkles near my face.

Even if you haven't gone gray like I have, chances are your hair has changed color a time or two (or three) by now. Also, as we age, our coloring softens and sometimes cools. So if you haven't had your colors done since back in the '80s, or ever, it might be a fun thing to try.

In a nutshell, seasonal color analysis is based on three things: how light/dark, bright/muted, and cool/warm your skin, hair, and eyes are. Based on your individual combination of these factors, you'll fit into one of four main palettes named for each of the four seasons. From there, you can break it down even further. You might be a Warm, Light, or Clear Spring. A Warm, Soft, or Deep Autumn. A Soft, Light or Cool Summer. A Deep, Cool or Clear Winter.

Some colors make us look tired, less vibrant, older. When we wear them, people see what we're wearing, while we disappear into the background. Finding the colors that work for us lets us be the star, not our clothing, which can make us look and feel awesome.

You can Google up seasonal color theory to find websites to help you figure out your own personal colors. (prettyyourworld.com is a good place to start.)

Or you can hire a seasonal color consultant to do your colors online or in person. If you manage to find someone local, you can even invite some friends and turn it into a party.

Seasonal color analysis is a great tool, though obviously if you don't like a color, or like the way a color looks or feels on you, you don't have to wear it just because you're a Warm Spring or a Deep Autumn. Still, for me, revisiting seasonal color theory after all these years is not only fun but it's helped simplify my life. When I walk into a store, I can go right for the colors I know will work.

And when I find something awesome in yellow or orange, I can alert a friend who could actually wear it!

Sister Brows

"No matter how plain a woman may be," Eleanor Roosevelt said, "if truth and honesty are written across her face, she will be beautiful."

It also helps to have good eyebrows. Eyes might be the windows to the soul, but our eyebrows frame those windows, adding shape and definition. So if our eyebrows aren't working for us, it's hard to see past them.

Eyebrows thin and lighten as we age. By midlife, lots of us are dealing with eyebrow problems.

I don't know about you, but like many other issues in my life, my wonky eyebrows were probably helped along by my perfectionism. You know, pluck a few hairs from the left brow to make it look more like the right. Then grab that yucky thick hair that just sprouted in the middle of the right brow. And wouldn't you know it, that just left a gap which makes the right eyebrow arch higher. So what can you do but pluck a few thinner hairs on the left side to try to balance things out.

And then one day we awake to discover we're seriously overplucked. Suddenly we understand how Great Aunt Dee Dee ended up drawing two half circles with orangey eye pencil where her eyebrows used to be and calling it a day.

Embracing our imperfection is a big part of shining on. Our eyebrows, like our breasts and our feet, aren't meant to be identical. They're supposed to be more like sisters, the eyebrow experts say, rather than twins. The sooner we face the fact that they're never going to be a perfect match, the better off we'll be.

The experts agree that one of the biggest mistakes midlife women make is to let their eyebrows get too thin. While we don't want to overdo it by trying to recreate our Brooke Shields eyebrows of the '80s, fuller eyebrows say young and healthy and vibrant. As we age, we should go easy on the plucking—less is far less likely to lead to disaster.

Get a strong magnifying mirror if you don't already have one, lighted if possible. And while you're checking out your brows, take a good look around the rest of your face, too. It seems cruel that just as our vision is starting to go, random hairs we might miss start sprouting on our chins. (Sorry to freak you out if you're not there yet!) Nobody likes to talk about it, but nothing says old like not dealing with them. So pluck, wax, or get laser hair removal treatments. Some dermatologists even recommend a quick spot shave, which is not as rough on the skin and also exfoliates.

As I research, I learn that our eyebrows grow in three to four month cycles of anagen, catagen, and telogen, which basically means that different hairs grow at different times. So if we want to reinvent our eyebrows, we've got to leave them alone through all three stages to give them time to grow back. Which means no plucking or waxing or threading at all.

I'm thinking it's probably too late for my own brows, but I give it a try. Maybe it's all that coconut oil I've been slathering on. Maybe the way I'm eating has kicked my thyroid into gear. (An underactive thyroid can cause the outer third of our eyebrows to thin or even disappear completely.) Whatever the cause, my eyebrows actually grow back. They're still not great, but they're much better.

Making our eyebrows too matchy-matchy with the color we dye our hair (a shade or two darker looks less fake), or too dark, or bleaching our eyebrows with facial bleach to make them lighter, can get us into trouble. Eyebrows that blend in rather than jump out are more forgiving. I track down a great chart to help us choose the right eyebrow shade based on our hair and skin color: http://www.ulta.com/shade-finders/anastasia-beverly-hills-shade-chart/.

You can get your eyebrows tinted, but chances are you'll still have to do some filling in. The best advice I find is to use an eyebrow pencil to outline your brows (short, light, imperfect lines so they don't look drawn on) the way you want them to be, remembering they're supposed to be similar, not identical. You can cheat the outline a bit to make them a tiny bit fuller. Just ignore the bald spots as well as any random hairs growing out there in no woman's land for now.

Once you finish outlining, fill in your brows with a good brow powder and then lock them in place with a clear brow gel.

Only then do you pick up the tweezers. And you pluck just the hairs that are growing outside the shapes you've created, and leave everything else alone. It's genius. And I never would have thought of it.

I try a few different options, but Anastasia brow products work best for me. I find a medium brown shade without a hint of orange that's perfect for me. The brow powder and pencil and gel are expensive, at least by my standards, but buying them as part of a kit cuts the price in half. There are plenty of other options out there, too. Friends of mine like Smashbox Brow Tech to Go and Maybelline Expert Eyes brow pencils.

The experts agree that as you continue to refine the shape of your eyebrows, go slowly. Brush your brows up and trim off the hairs that reach past the rest of your eyebrows with small scissors if you need to. You can make your midlife eyes look less hooded and droopy by gently arching your brows a bit, and by lifting the underside closest to your nose with a little cautious plucking, so they don't have that comma look. If the outer end of your eyebrows curves down toward your eyes, giving you a hangdog expression, you can reshape until the line is a bit straighter and stretches out toward your temples.

If you can find a good brow artist to help you out, it might be worth it. I wouldn't mind finding one myself. But besides the damage I've done solo, I've had my eyebrows butchered several times over the years by well-intended professionals. So it feels good to learn how to make the most of my imperfect brows myself.

Have a Heart

I love found sculptures. Walking in the woods at Christmastime and discovering a scrubby little pine tree with candy canes hanging from it and a tinsel garland wrapped around it like a hug. Or strolling across the beach and finding all the left-behind flip-flops dangling from a mast-like hunk of driftwood.

Midlife Rocks is something I say all the time, so maybe that's where it starts. As I walk along the river path, I find myself stopping occasionally to make a pile of little flat rocks, each one smaller that the one it's perched on. I stack them on the ground, or on a boulder, or on a fallen moss-covered log, or even on a tree limb reaching out like an arm.

And then I keep walking. It's fun. It's zen. But mostly it's a gift. I hope that when other people notice one of my tiny rock sculptures, it will make them smile.

Then one day I find my first heart-shaped rock. It's maybe two inches in diameter and nestled on a bed of pine needles about a foot off the path. It's perfectly imperfect—undeniably shaped like a real heart, but more like *The Velveteen Rabbit* kind of real, as if it's been bumped around a bit and loved into shape by nature.

I know I should leave it to make someone else's day like it's just made mine, but apparently my midlife rocks generosity is limited. I can't do it.

Instead I use pebbles to create the shape of a heart around my found treasure. Then I pick up my heart-shaped rock and walk away.

In my head, Janis Joplin breaks into "Piece of My Heart," which doesn't help the guilt factor.

Confucius jumps in to make me feel better: "Wherever you go, go with all your heart."

And so a collection is born. I start seeing heart-shaped rocks everywhere. (I even find one embedded in the beach pebble tile on the floor of my shower.) Collecting them is another way of training my eyes to see. It's also a way of being present, not something that comes easily to me given my tendency to drift along with my head in my imaginary book world. It's inspiring. It's uplifting.

When I post a photo of one on Facebook, I find out I'm not the only one collecting heart-shaped rocks. Linda says finding one means I'm going to have a good day. Beth says a heart-shaped rock is nature's valentine. Janie says she has looked for heart-shaped rocks on beaches all over the world.

Elizabeth says that a friend of hers used to collect heart-shaped rocks. When she died, her kids gave each person at the funeral one of her rocks to take home to remember her by.

Deanell posts that just the night before, she was reading *Must Love Dogs: Fetch You Later*, where Sarah talks about finding a heart-shaped rock. It's my book and I don't even remember that part. So I look it up, and of course she's right: "I squatted down to pick up a perfectly heart-shaped beach pebble. The first time I'd found a heart-shaped rock as a little girl, I'd asked my mother if the ocean did this on purpose. I turned it over in my hand, still wondering."

I have absolutely no idea where that came from. It's freaky

how often my life imitates my fiction, as if a part of me knew all along that something was going to happen.

What I do know is that I've always had some ambivalence about hearts. Valentine's Day is my birthday. The doctor who delivered me tried to convince my parents to name me Valentina. I remember scratching my way through an entire birthday as a toddler wearing a puffy, itchy dress made out of red organza with white hearts. Heart-shaped lockets. Heart-shaped birthday cakes. Conversation hearts, gummy hearts, cinnamon hearts. When it came to my birthday, we had a theme.

On the one hand it's a great birthday to have, because people remember it. On the other hand, while it's definitely not as bad as a Christmas birthday, it's kind of a buy-one-get-one-free deal. Over the years, I think I've received every Happy Valentine's/Birthday card ever made.

As problems go, this is a good one to have. But still, no one is more surprised by my new heart obsession than I am. I see hearts everywhere. Bleeding heart flowers. The petals of a pansy. The heart-shaped leaves of redbud trees, elephant ear plants, violets, morning glories.

My heart-shaped jewelry disappeared during the robbery, but I dig up a scarf with hearts on it that someone gave me and wear it for the first time. The next time I'm in a store, I'm drawn to a white blouse covered in funky batik-like blue hearts. I leave without it, then drive all the way back to the store two days later to buy it.

Our collections can be lots of things. A way of creating a legacy. A way of comforting ourselves by accumulating. Sometimes it's the thrill of the hunt. Collecting can be a kind of obsession. The first step on the slippery slope to becoming a hoarder. A stress reliever. A way of reliving our childhoods. A competitive challenge. A way of bringing order to a disorderly world.

A friend of mine collects Hello Kitty memorabilia.

Another collects Elvis stuff. In my novel *Life's a Beach*, Ginger and Geri's parents collect a tiny bottle's worth of sand from every beach they visit. My mother collected buttons in little Whitman's Sampler boxes. My mother-in-law collected Hummel figurines.

Over the years, I've known people who've collected lava lamps, jewelry boxes, perfume bottles, antique bottles, snow globes, seashells, sea glass, egg cups, dice, salt and pepper shakers, cookbooks, autographed books, Pez candy dispensers, owls, frogs, feathers, thimbles, pitchers, Tarot cards, crystals, refrigerator magnets.

I think collections are fun. They give us a goal and the pleasure of achieving it. Even if we're simplifying our lives, collecting things can be a way of narrowing down what we want to hang on to. Our choices say a lot about who we are.

Displaying our collections can be another way of being creative. Under a glass bell jar. Inside an unused fireplace. Over a doorframe. In a shadowbox. Or an old wooden chicken feeder. Or a vintage wood typeset printing letter drawer.

I arrange my heart-shaped rocks on a shelf so I'll see them every time I walk into my office. When one of my cats bats one off the edge, it breaks in half as it hits the floor. Oh, well, I've certainly had bigger broken hearts in my lifetime.

Who knows why hearts suddenly speak to me. Maybe I'm remembering who I've been all along. Maybe it's about who I'm becoming.

Out of the blue I recall that when I wrote my novel *Wallflower in Bloom*, I began each chapter with a chiasmus—two parallel phrases with a reversal in the order of words. So I make up a chiasmus for my new collection and write it in my Shine On notebook:

You can't have a rock-shaped heart

while looking for heart-shaped rocks.

If you're feeling a chiasmus coming on, write it in your Shine On notebook. And/or right here:

____

____

Makeup Wakeup

"Beauty is part facial symmetry, part surprise, part attitude," says Bella, my makeup artist heroine in *Summer Blowout*. I think Bella would be the first to tell us that one of the best ways to feel beautiful at midlife is to stay in the moment and not compare the way we look now with the way we used to look.

And also to ditch all that old makeup that's not working for us anymore!

I'm embarrassed to say how long most of my own makeup has been kicking around, so I grab a tall kitchen trash bag and shovel everything in but my new eyebrow stuff. Fast, before I start hanging on to things just in case.

I have a great, informative conversation with my friend Charlotte Phinney, a hair and makeup stylist whose list of celebrity and non-celebrity clients is a mile long. I Google up everything I can find. I log lots of research hours reading blogs and watching makeup tutorials for midlife women on YouTube.

I talk to other women, too, both in person and online. Some of them are over makeup completely now. Many of them still want to wear at least some makeup, at least sometimes, but they're at a loss as to what works for their changing faces and skin. I hear stories of frustration, that just when they find a formula or color they like, it changes or gets discontinued. So there's plenty of annoyance and not much brand loyalty when it comes to midlife makeup. Just about everyone I talk to asks me to get back to them if I come across any good products.

When it comes to makeup, the experts agree that it's important to bring color to our cheeks and lips as we age. Some say that once we reach midlife, we should always use a cream blush. Others say a powder blush works fine as long as it contains brighteners. On the fictional side, Bella from *Summer Blowout* thinks Nars blush in Orgasm looks great on just about everyone, though I'm pretty sure what she likes best about it is the name.

One expert says our lipstick should be two shades darker than our natural lip color. Another says that it should match our inner lips or gums. Still another says nudes and neutrals will make us look washed out as we get older, and pink is always better for fair skin, berry colors for medium skin, and deeper shades like plum for dark skin. Some experts say darker lipsticks make our midlife lips look too thin. Others warn us to beware of anything too shiny. Or not shiny enough.

Just as I'm starting to get a makeup headache, I realize that the only way to figure out what looks good on me and what doesn't is to try it.

There are some terrific makeup artists at salons, as well as freelancers you can hire to give you a makeover or a makeup class for a fee. You can also find some great makeup professionals at department store makeup counters and beauty product stores who will do your makeup without charging. Though it's important to know that management has sales quotas for these employees, so the expectation is that when they spend their valuable time with you, you'll buy products.

I'd like to avoid ending up with makeup that I don't really

want. I find out that lots of chain drugstores will let you return products that don't work for you, even if you've opened them. But I don't want to have to buy before I try.

What I really want to do is try with no pressure to buy. My local Ulta turns out to be a great find. They even provide disposable applicators and alcohol wipes to clean off the trial products. And good makeup mirrors. (Friends of mine swear by Sephora for trying makeup, but it's a longer drive for me.)

So whenever I have some extra time, I head for Ulta and grab a bar stool in the makeup section. I open a fresh page in my Shine On notebook and draw an oval on it, which I divide down the middle. I divide my real face down the middle, too, with an imaginary line. Then I make up each side of my face with different products and record them in the notebook so I don't forget what I've tried and where.

It's fun. Mostly I'm ignored, and nobody tries to sell me anything. Sometimes I chat with another woman and we share suggestions. Occasionally an employee asks me if I need any help. When I tell her I'm all set, she moves on to the next person.

I discover CC (color correcting) cream, which contains primer, foundation, concealer, brightener, and SPF protection all rolled into one. Using each of these products separately might work better, but I know I'll never take the time. I want simple, something that's one and done. It Cosmetics Your Skin But Better CC Cream with SPF 50+ turns out to be a good choice for me. I try it in different shades, narrow it down to the shade that disappears at my chin line, and check to see if it still looks good a few hours later, and a few hours after that. Only then do I by it. Friends recommend Lumene Time Freeze Anti-Age Color Correcting CC Cream and Olay Total Effects CC Tone Correcting UV Moisturizer, if you're looking for others to try.

I hit some more beauty supply stores as well as department stores. I discover that cream blushes work best for me now.

Bobbi Brown Pot Rouge for Lips and Cheeks is a good one to try, especially since you can simplify further by using one product on both your cheeks and lips. Nars makes The Multiple, a color stick that you can use on your cheeks, lips, and eyes—and yes, it comes in Orgasm. Women I talk to like MAC Cremeblend blush, Tarte Cheek Stain, and Maybelline Dream Bouncy Blush.

Moisturizing lipsticks and crayons turn out to be my best bet for my lips. I love Laura Geller moisturizing lip crayon in Love Me Dew and Tarte's LipSurgence Lip Crème in Empowered. Women I talk to like CoverGirl Lip Perfection Lip Color and Clinique Chubby Stick Intense Moisturizing Lip Color Balm.

The experts agree that a lip pencil, clear or the color of our lips, will keep our lipstick from bleeding into those vertical lines that start to appear around our lips at midlife. I've never tried a clear lip pencil before, and I find it works much better for me than a colored lip liner, which has a tendency to hang around and look weird once my lipstick fades away. Paula's Choice makes a good clear lip liner.

Thinning eyelashes are a part of the aging process. I'm surprised to find out what a difference curling them can make, since I didn't think I had enough left to curl. I find a Japonesque Go Curl pocket curler that works better and is much easier to use than the ancient drugstore model I just threw out.

Makeup Forever and Revlon Colorstay eyeliners both work well for me and are soft enough to be gentle on the sensitive skin around my eyes. Charcoal is a better eyeliner color on me now than brown. Neutrogena Nourishing Long Wear eye shadow has a built-in primer and comes in a soft cool taupe palette that works for me. I don't find a mascara I like better than Maybelline Great Lash, so I buy a new one to replace the tube I've tossed.

One of my best finds is Laura Geller Baked Portofino

Highlighter. As a final step in my simplified makeup routine, I brush it lightly under my eyebrows, as well as on my tear ducts, the top of my cheeks, my forehead, my chin, down the length of my nose.

You're glowing, people say to me.

Which I like to think is another way of saying I'm shining on.

Yoga Fail

In my quest to try new things and figure out which ones I like, I decide to sample some of the classes offered at my gym.

I want to love yoga, I really do. I've tried it a few times over the years, and it just wasn't my thing. It's like that book everyone raves to you about, but even though they think it's the best book ever written, you can't get into it. I'd spend most of the class watching the clock and wishing I were taking something a little more fun and upbeat.

I find lots of good reasons to give yoga another try. Yoga can help relieve our stress as well as our anxiety. It can improve our strength, flexibility, and posture. There's even evidence that yoga can help manage high blood pressure and ease pain. And, who knows, maybe this time around I'll actually love it.

After checking out the yoga options on the class schedule, I choose a Vinyasa yoga class partly because it's a beginner's level class and also because the description says that this kind of yoga focuses on using the breath as a guide to flow from one posture to the next. I have a tendency to breathe shallowly, and I've noticed that sometimes I even hold my breath when I'm really concentrating on something, which I realize

I'm doing only when I start to get dizzy. So it seems like Vinyasa yoga might be a good choice for me.

When I arrive, I roll out a yoga mat in an inconspicuous spot near the back of the room, kick off my flip-flops, sit down on the mat, cross my legs. It's a large bright studio with shiny wooden floors and multiple paddle fans twirling from the high ceiling. I look around the room to check out the other participants. Mostly women. A mix of ages. I'm moderately intimidated as I am by every new activity, but it's not too bad. I roll my shoulders back, take a few deep breaths.

And then the class starts.

Apparently the instructor hasn't read the description of her own class, or noticed that this is supposed to be a class for beginners. Within minutes there's a lot more panting than breathing going on. I flash back to that '80s movie *Private Benjamin*, when Goldie Hawn realizes she's joined the wrong army and it's not the one with the condos and the private rooms. *Wait*, I want to yell. *I did join the yoga class but I joined a different yoga class. The one where the beginners all just sit around and breathe.*

I lose count after maybe the 40th plank. By the 19th or 20th downward dog, I'm ready to roll over and play dead. Eventually I sink back into a child's pose, close my eyes, resist the urge to start sucking my thumb. I'm hoping I can get away with not moving again until this hell on earth is over. I feel beaten down, inadequate, less than. Like my best days are behind me.

I feel old.

When I look up, the instructor is doing a side crow, hands on the floor, feet off the ground, both knees balanced on the triceps of one arm. Seriously. Then she kicks her legs out in the air and holds the pose. I look around the room. Maybe two people are trying to keep up with her, but everybody else looks disheartened. Depressed. One woman is rubbing her shoulder. Another has rolled over to her back and is staring up at the ceiling.

Suddenly I'm pissed. I'm not old. I'm just too old for this sh*t.

I don't even wait until class is over to escape—I head for the hills during the water break. I do a couple of fast, soothing laps around the indoor track and then I saunter into the stretching room.

There's that Buddhist proverb that when the student is ready, the teacher will appear. Maybe I wasn't ready to like yoga. Maybe I never will be.

But one thing I know is that when we're trying to learn something, the right teacher can make all the difference. And when you're a teacher, it doesn't matter how good you are at something. It doesn't matter if you get bored with the easier poses, or you'd like to get your own yoga practice in. Your job is to start where your students are and guide them to the next level, all the while making them feel that anything is possible. When you're a teacher, it's not about you—it's about your students.

If you find yourself in a class of any kind that makes you feel bad, get out. Life's too short to spend it watching show-off yoga. Or show-off anything. I even think our job is to protect ourselves from this kind of thing if we can. These experiences are definitely not the path to shining on.

I know there are plenty of great yoga teachers out there, probably even at my gym, and I could just keep looking until I find the right one. But we don't have time to do it all, even if we want to, and I decide I've given yoga enough chances, at least for now.

There's No Place Like Om

There's a bright side to everything, even abandoned yoga classes. It hits me as I'm driving home from the gym that what I find appealing about yoga is the meditative aspect.

And I've already been meditating since I was 17.

When I was a junior in high school, a very cool psychology teacher received a grant to pay for a group of sophomores and juniors to receive training in transcendental meditation. The academic progress of these students would then be measured against another group of students who didn't meditate.

In a lucky break that I know I didn't appreciate enough at the time, I was one of the students chosen to get the training. This was not necessarily a compliment. Hindsight 20/20, I'm pretty sure I was flagged because, even though I was still pretty much holding my own in the honors classes, I'd gone over to the other side and started hanging out with the wild kids. What can I say, they were fun.

So one Saturday another chosen student and I carpool to a hall a half-hour away to learn transcendental meditation, aka TM. About halfway there we remember we're supposed to bring flowers, so we pull off the road and pick a bouquet of what may or may not have been ragweed.

I don't remember what happens with the flowers. We sit on pillows on the floor with some other people. The instructor takes us each aside and gives us our individual mantra, a couple of Sanskrit syllables that we're told we're not supposed to share with anyone. Then we do a group meditation. The instructor tells us all to meditate twice a day for 20 minutes. Unless we're under 20—then we'll meditate for 17 minutes while we're 17, 18 minutes while we're 18, etc. until we're 20. This seems like an awful lot of math for a Saturday.

When we're back in the car again, my carpool buddy, whose name is Donna, turns to me and says, "I don't get it."

The following Saturday we drive to the same hall for a TM checkup and another group meditation. When we get back out to the car, Donna says, "I still don't get it."

About 25 years later, Donna and I run into each other again. "You know, I never did get it," she says. I know immediately what she's talking about, and we both crack up.

But I took to transcendental meditation right away. TM is a simple technique that calms us into a kind of a restful alertness. It's a great tool to settle our minds, to help us cope with stress, to access our creativity. Studies have shown that transcendental meditation can reduce depression and post traumatic stress syndrome. It can lower our blood pressure and help us sleep better. It can improve our concentration and give us a greater sense of well-being.

To do TM, you just sit in a chair or lean back against the headboard while you're sitting up in bed. You close your eyes and let your head drop forward comfortably. Then you think of your mantra, which helps you sink into a meditative state. When your mind drifts, you let it go, and then gently bring it back to the mantra.

It always sounds so hippy dippy when I try to describe it. But it's not. It's also not about mental discipline or concentration or chanting or anything mystical. It's not about being mindful. You don't try to control your breathing, or your muscles, or your thoughts.

I once heard TM described as a kind of self-hypnosis, with the mantra being the trigger instead of a pocket watch swinging back and forth.

I've been doing TM for most of my life now, and the biggest thing I think it does for me is to allow me to better tap into my creativity, kind of like sinking past all the noise so my brain can find the ideas that are floating around inside of me and make stronger, more interesting connections. TM is also soothing and restful, and meditating makes me feel so much better when I'm under a lot of stress, or I haven't had enough sleep and need to function.

The Beatles were the first famous advocates of transcendental meditation. "In moments of madness, meditation has helped me find moments of serenity," Paul McCartney has said. Other celebrities who practice TM include Sheryl Crow, Jennifer Aniston, Hugh Jackman, Cameron Diaz, Robin Roberts, Laura Dern, Clint Eastwood, Jerry Seinfeld, Martin Scorsese and many, many more.

Maybe I'm missing something, but what I don't understand is why transcendental meditation training is so expensive—around $1500 as of this writing—which may not be a big deal for Hollywood celebs, but it's a lot of money for most of the midlife women I know. TM is a simple technique that's just not that hard to do. I've even tried using "beach" as my mantra instead of my secret Sanskrit syllables and it works just fine.

So you might want to try meditating on your own, or Google up some articles and tutorials first before you plunk down your money. There are lots of other kinds of meditation you can look into, too, from mindful meditation to guided meditation. Prayer can be a kind of meditation, too.

Or you can always take a yoga class. Just don't expect to run into me there!

Get Out, Way Out

"We choose our life by how we spend our time," John Maxwell said.

"Why do you stay in prison/When the door is so wide open?" Rumi said.

According to the Environmental Protection Agency, the average American spends 93% of his or her life indoors—87% in a building and 6% in a car.

I love spending time outdoors, and I definitely don't do enough of it. So I head off to enjoy one of my favorite outdoor activities, kayaking.

If you've never tried it, kayaking is so much fun. I don't own my own kayak, mostly because I know it would only turn into one of those things that takes up space in the garage and makes me feel guilty that I'm not using it enough.

If you Google kayaking and your zip code, you'll find the nearest place to rent a kayak. I also found a meetup.com group in my area that offers classes for beginners who'd like to learn how to kayak and want some help getting started, as well as kayaking get-togethers for people looking for some company.

I think kayaking is a great sport for midlife women. We don't have to be super-athletic or coordinated to do it. It improves our core and upper body strength. It's a great way to spend time in nature.

When it comes to kayaking, you don't have to be a daredevil. I like short recreational kayaks with deep, roomy cockpits that make them easy to get in and out of. I prefer rowing on the flat water of a lake, a tranquil stretch of river, a sheltered ocean bay. I keep my rental life jacket buckled up at all times.

So I rent a kayak at the rental place closest to my house, right next to the river. A college-age kid drags it down to the water for me, waits while I get settled in, gives me a whistle to blow in case I need help or a tow back to the rental place, pushes me out into the water.

A few strokes in, I feel like I'm miles away from everything, even though in reality I'm just off a busy street. I paddle past a line of turtles basking in the sun on a log. A gaggle of geese hanging out on a tiny island in the middle of the river. A great blue heron fishing up a snack.

As I paddle, the underused muscles in my arms and back start to burn a bit, but in a good way. My abs are definitely getting a workout, too.

I feel strong. I feel invincible. Helen Reddy even starts singing "I Am Woman."

A line from the movie *Deliverance* pops into my head: "Sometimes you've got to lose yourself to find yourself."

My head clears. I'm calmer. Serene. Tranquil. I make a vow to get away from civilization like this more often.

And then I look over the side of my kayak. Not only can I see the bottom of the river through the tea-colored water, but when I touch it with my paddle, which isn't all that long, most of the paddle is still above water. I'm pretty sure I've had deeper water in my bathtub.

So much for my wild river adventure. If I get tired of paddling, I could jump out and river-walk my way back to the rental place, dragging my kayak behind me.

And then I remember an African proverb: "Only a fool tests the depth of the water with both feet."

Daft for Crafts

I'm feeling crafty. And maybe I should pretend that I have an urge to make sea glass earrings like Ginger does in *Life's a Beach*. Or take up metal sculpting like Melanie does in *Time Flies*. Or build an entire sofa from wooden pallets with one hand tied behind my back.

But the truth is I've been collecting wine corks for a long time, and along with my trusty glue gun, they're calling out to me.

There, I said it. We shouldn't have to justify our creative impulses or make excuses for them. If it sounds like fun, why not just get our craft on and give it a whirl? So what if we're called to sew a squirrel costume for our dog, or crochet a Barbie doll dress with a hooped skirt that fits over that backup roll of toilet paper. Who are we to judge that hand-painted Barry Manilow tie. Or the napkin holders made out of old socks.

I think of our creativity as a muscle. Crafting is one more way to strengthen that muscle, to challenge ourselves, to try something new. Completing craft projects gives us a sense of accomplishment, especially if we're pleased with the results. And hopefully a few good laughs if we're not so pleased.

When it comes to crafting, I tend to have great vision, but the implementation of that vision—not so much. Apparently I'm not alone, since there are pictures of failed craft projects all over the Internet. I've blocked most of my own failures, but I do remember once making a king-sized quilt out of squares of fabric cut from old clothing. I could see this amazing creation so clearly in my head. But when I finally managed to finish it, the squares didn't even come close to lining up the way they were supposed to, and the quilt weighed about 200 pounds. It was definitely warm, though, I'll give it that.

Years ago my stepmother made us a Humpty Dumpty-like stuffed Santa with long skinny legs and a red velvet hat, and it's still the first decoration we take out every year at Christmas. Friends have knitted scarves for me, and I love that every time I wear one it makes me think of that friend.

The repetition of crafting is soothing, even meditative. Finding that place of flow quiets our anxiety. Crafting increases our attention span. It exercises our problem-solving abilities. It can help stimulate memories. One study even found that activities like crafting could reduce our chances of developing mild cognitive impairment by 30 to 50%.

But back to the wine corks. I start collecting them in a big clear rectangular glass vase that sits on the brick fireplace hearth in our kitchen. I'm not sure why—I guess I just like the way they look in there.

When they find out I'm saving wine corks, some friends and family members start saving them for me, too. One, who works in the wine and spirits industry, donates a big bag of corks to the cause.

So I've got plenty of wine corks to work with. A quick stroll through the crafts blogs tells me that there are lots of options for using them, too, everything from wine cork planters to wine cork jewelry organizers to wine cork bathmats. Wine cork crafts have been around since the 1950s. And apparently they're a thing again.

I find some great cork wreaths on Pinterest, so my first thought is to make one for my front door. I'm okay with the message this might send to our letter carrier, but I decide I don't want to deal with the possibility of glue-gunned corks popping off the wreath and rolling around all over the place when the door slams.

I finally decide to make a wine cork bulletin board. Even though I make most of my notes in one of my notebooks or in Word documents, I could use a place in my office to tack Post-Its scribbled with things I don't want to forget.

The easiest thing to do would be to go to a crafts store and buy something—maybe a shadow box—and glue the corks onto the bottom of that. But I want to upcycle something vintage instead, so I head for a thrift store. I think I'm looking for a deep picture frame or a funky old mirror.

What I find instead is a square tortoiseshell tray with two handles cut into the sides. It's got a few scratches. Not only do I think they add to its charm, but the scratches make me feel less guilty about gluing wine corks all over the tray.

Once my glue gun heats up, I start covering the bottom of the tray with corks. I make a pattern with two corks going vertically, then two corks going horizontally, as if I were laying out a brick walkway. It's fun. It's relaxing. It reawakens my creativity. Visions of craftiness dance in my head—maybe I'll make that wine cork wreath after all. And I just saw a tutorial for a funky infinity scarf made out of an old T-shirt.

When I finish making it, I hang my wine cork bulletin board on a wall in my office. I'm thrilled with the way it came out. I love the idea that I can take it down and use it as a tray, too.

Instead of Post-Its, I find myself tacking photos on my wine cork creation. A photo of a simple screened porch I printed out in case we ever get around to screening in our back deck. A picture of a turquoise beach cruiser bike I clipped from a brochure to remind me how much I love riding bikes on the beach. A photo of a gorgeous purple field of lavender to remind me that I'd like to write another adventure for the women of *The Wildwater Walking Club*. A picture of the perfect little beach bungalow, maybe a future vacation rental, maybe a future home if proximity to the ocean wins out after all.

I realize I'm creating a vision board, a collage of things I'd like to do, maybe even to attract into my life. I've never taken the time to make one before. As I keep adding photos, I realize that it's helping me get clear about what I want. I think having the images in front of me, instead of buried in a pile on my desk, might also keep me from forgetting about them or getting sidetracked. I make a rudimentary sketch of a book, add the title of the book I'm working on, tack it onto a cork in the middle of the board. I print out another copy of my Shine On word cloud and tack it next to the book.

Whenever I look at my wine cork vision board, it makes me happy. And I'm reminded once again that, for me, taking the time to try something crafty, or do anything creative, always makes my life better.

Sweet Dreams

My wine cork collection has dwindled. It's not being replenished very quickly either. While my life is not completely corkless, there's not very much alcohol-drinking going on these days, wine or otherwise. I'm not sure whether my new way of eating is a factor, but I've definitely become way more sensitive to alcohol. A glass of red wine at dinner sometimes means that, even if I fall right to sleep as soon as my head hits the pillow, I usually wake up a few hours later and then toss and turn for the rest of the night.

Bummer. I love the idea of having a glass of wine to reward myself for all my hard work, a day well lived. It seems like such a civilized custom. Red wine contains resveratrol, for goodness sake, which is supposed to be great for you. Studies show that light alcohol consumption can improve our episodic memory, which is the ability to recall events. I'm a writer—I need to remember stuff. And even if the pendulum swings in the opposite direction and a study comes out tomorrow saying that alcohol is, in fact, not even the tiniest bit good for us, I hardly have any vices left. Surely we're all entitled to hang onto a few so we don't get too boring.

Other midlife women I know tell me they've become more

sensitive to alcohol, too. One says her face flushes red as soon as she has a drink, something she definitely doesn't need when she's already dealing with hot flashes. Another wakes up with a brutal headache the next day whenever she drinks even a small amount of wine.

And wouldn't you know it, I've recently stumbled on a really cool thing to do with wine corks, too, something I wish I'd started doing decades ago. It's a kind of wine cork journaling—I mean, how brilliant is that. When you open a special bottle of wine, you use a permanent marker to write the date, the place, as well as who you shared the wine with and/or what the occasion was. Then you collect the wine corks in a beautiful bowl or a vintage wire basket, or a tall clear glass vase like the one I have on my kitchen hearth. I think it would be so much fun to go through the corks that we've collected over the years every once in a while to trigger all those half-forgotten memories.

But as far as I'm concerned, anything that gets in the way of a restful night's sleep needs to be avoided at all costs, even the artful accumulation of corks. Sleep-deprivation sucks. And it's been linked to everything from obesity to heart disease to a higher injury rate.

When it comes to the ultimate luxury, it's tough to top a good night's sleep. Sufficient sleep can help us think more clearly, feel more optimistic. It even improves our memory—probably much more than that glass of wine, much as it pains me to admit it—because while we sleep, our brain processes our activities of the day and stores them in our memory banks. The experts say sleep and metabolism are controlled by the same parts of the brain, which is why we feel less hungry when we get more sleep and want to eat everything in sight when we're sleep-deprived.

"A good laugh and a long sleep are the best cures in the doctor's book," an Irish proverb says.

Even the Dalai Lama said, "Sleep is the best meditation."

Sleep may enhance the creative process. And research shows that if we have a big decision to make, the best thing to do is to sleep on it first, because sleep gets our subconscious involved in helping us process all the variables.

Experts recommend we get seven to nine hours of sleep each night. If we're having a hard time achieving that, besides forgoing the alcohol, we can try cutting out caffeine at noon. (I don't know about you, but I'm definitely more sensitive to caffeine now, too.) We should make sure our bedrooms are as dark as possible when we sleep, too—I've even started covering my digital alarm clock with a scarf at night.

I've also splurged on a 100% silk pillowcase, which I often dot with a few drops of lavender essential oil. The silk helps keep me cool while I sleep—I don't have to keep flipping the pillow to find a cooler side the way I do with a cotton pillowcase. A silk pillowcase is also easier on my curls as well as on my skin, so I don't wake up with bedhead and pillowcase wrinkles pressed into my face.

I've always heard that a hot bath helps you sleep, but I recently read that taking a hot bath too close to bedtime might actually impair our sleep, because our body temperature has to drop to a certain level to sleep soundly. Who knows—but it's definitely one more thing to consider if you're having trouble sleeping. I do know that I sleep better in a cool room and keep the paddle fan going over the bed at night year round.

The experts say the optimum temperature for sleeping varies for individuals but is somewhere between 60 and 68 degrees.

I've learned the hard way not to check email, open snail mail, read texts, or answer the phone right before I go to bed. It just winds me up and gets my mind racing. Unless I'm waiting for something I have to deal with immediately, I try to shut down my computer at least an hour before I go to bed, and I also let the phone go to voicemail unless I think it might be some kind of emergency.

Keeping the bedroom clutter-free helps, too, as well as making it a TV-free zone. A bedtime snack of yogurt, cheese, nuts, seeds, turkey or other foods high in tryptophan can also help us sleep better.

I go to bed at the same ridiculously early time (9-ish) whenever I can, because I love getting up early (5-ish) and working before the rest of the world wakes up. And because going to bed at the same time every night helps our body set its internal clock. And also because my cats are ridiculously early risers and they don't have snooze buttons.

A recent study found that people who do their pre-bedtime reading on an iPad or other ebook reader with an illuminated screen took 10 minutes longer to fall asleep. These people also had significantly less REM deep sleep during the course of the night and found it harder to fully wake up the next morning. Scientists think the bluish light from the electronics might have an impact on our brains.

I always read in bed before I go to sleep, so I've started reading a paper book whenever I can. But if I'm in the middle of a good ebook and want to keep going, I have a pretty nifty trick.

This is how I discovered it: Not long ago I'm starting to have symptoms of eyestrain that I'm pretty sure are caused, at least in part, by the glare on my computer screen. I scroll through message boards for possible solutions, trying to decide whether I should order a special anti-glare film for my computer screen, or if I should just cut to the chase and think about upgrading my computer to one that has an anti-glare screen.

And I stumble on a post by this midlife woman, whose name I'm so sorry I don't remember, saying that she started wearing her reading sunglasses at her computer and she hasn't had a problem with eyestrain since. I buy my reading glasses in bulk because I'm always losing them, and each "collection" includes a pair of reading sunglasses, which I never wear because I don't read in the sun. So I dig up a pair of these sunglass cheaters and start wearing them at the computer. It works perfectly—no glare on the screen, no eyestrain. Total genius.

So now I've started using my reading sunglasses when I read on my iPad at night. I don't have any trouble sleeping, and it also makes my whole bedroom look darker, which sleep experts say is an important signal to our biological clock that we're getting ready for sleep. I'm sure I look bizarre wearing sunglasses in bed, but nobody sees me except Jake, who has seen me do far stranger things.

While I still have a glass of wine or two every once in a while, I weigh it against the cost of a potentially sleepless night. Occasionally, it's totally worth it—most of the time it's not. As for wine cork journaling, I guess I'll just have to save it for one of my fictional characters down the road.

Sometimes we do everything right and sleep still eludes us. Maybe the best thing to do then is to remember this advice from Rumi: "The breeze at dawn has secrets to tell you. Do not go back to sleep."

Maybe I'm just a contrarian, but it puts me back to sleep every time.

Who, Me?

So this woman I know got all freaked out when she dropped in for a haircut at a walk-in place. It happened to be senior discount day and the hair stylist gave her, *gasp*, the senior discount. That this woman had probably qualified for the senior discount a few years earlier didn't seem to factor into the equation for her.

One of my favorite cashiers at the grocery store told me senior discount day can be a delicate dance. On the one hand, people get mad if you don't give them the discount. On the other hand, they're pissed that you think they're old enough to qualify. When I asked her how she handles it, she said she just gives it to everybody who looks old enough and keeps her mouth shut. So I asked her how she knows who's old enough for the discount, which is 55 at this store.

Oh, she said, *it's not that hard to tell.*

Here's the thing: When it comes to our ages, we're not kidding anyone, except maybe ourselves. Even if we color our hair, get oodles of plastic surgery, wear three sets of shapewear, and have killer genes, there will be some telltale sign of our chronological age—our chin, our neck, the veins on the back of our hands. That doesn't mean we don't look good. But it doesn't mean we don't look our age either.

So maybe the thing we really need to do is get over ourselves.

Nobody else cares. The kid at the movie theater who just sold us a ticket doesn't care how old we are. He's just waiting for us to go away so he can text his girlfriend. The cashier at the grocery store just doesn't want us to yell at her for giving us the senior discount, or for not giving us the senior discount.

It's only a big deal if we make it a big deal.

I also think we have a tremendous opportunity, and maybe even a little bit of a responsibility, to reinvent every age we're fortunate enough to attain for the women coming up behind us. I can't tell you how much it inspires me to hear that Annie Lennox is 60, or Bonnie Raitt is 65, or Meryl Streep is 66, or Kathy Bates is 67, or Patti Smith is 68, or Diane Keaton and Sally Field are 69, or Helen Mirren and Debbie Harry and Goldie Hawn are 70, or Blythe Danner is 72, or Lily Tomlin is 76, or Jane Fonda is 77, or Maggie Smith is 80, or Gloria Steinem and Jane Goodall and Shirley MacLaine are 81, or Joanne Woodward is 85, or Betty White is 93.

When I hear other women's ages, it opens the door to new possibilities for me. Sure we're living in a youth-obsessed culture, but who cares? I'm so okay with being 83 someday if I can rock it like that 83-year-old woman at my gym who can leg press 180 pounds. That woman has reinvented 83 for me.

And I think it would be great to have younger women look up to me this way, too. To feel that their lives won't be over when they get to be my age. In fact, they'll be just getting up to speed.

We can all choose to become role models for how to grow awesome instead of old, each in our own unique and authentic way. But this is a lot harder to do if we don't own our age and rock it proudly.

I also think it might help if we all stop telling one another how young we look for our age. I'm the worst—I do it all the time. But my experience has been that when another midlife woman tells me how old she is, she's usually waiting for me to tell her she doesn't look that old. So I jump right in, because I don't think any of us get enough compliments, and I love to give them. *Ohmigod*, I say, *you'd never guess. You look so young for your age.*

I'm working on coming up with better things to say. *Good for you. You have the best smile. I love your tattoo.* Because when it comes to compliments, I don't think *you look so young* is helping any of us. There are so many more interesting things about us than looking young for our age.

Getting back to the senior discount, some people advise us to refuse it. They say taking it will make us feel older, less than. That if we take it, we're participating in ageism. We're letting our age define and limit us.

Your life, your choice. And if you don't need any extra money, good for you. But for the rest of us, here's what I think: We should take that freakin' senior discount and run. (Heads up: 50 is the new 65 when it comes to senior discounts, so Google around to see what's out there.) We've earned that discount, just by virtue of surviving this long, like making it through a whole bunch of elimination rounds on a TV reality show. And even if we don't really deserve it just for persistence in existence, so what, we should take it anyway. I mean, how often in life does free money come along?

Whatever you save—5% at the movie theater or grocery store, 10% on a gym membership or a car rental or a hotel room—put that same amount of money into a Shine On fund. Keep going until you have enough money to take a trip. Or a class. Or to buy a great big canvas and some bottles of acrylic paint to drip all over it.

If you're not there yet, I'm not saying you should lie about your age just to get the senior discount, although that might be a fun twist! But as soon as we qualify, I think we should not only take it—but we should use it to help us grow awesome instead of old.

Our SuperShero Power

Under the guise of research, I'm binge-watching *Grace and Frankie*, the Netflix series starring Jane Fonda and Lily Tomlin. It's slow to grab me, but by about the third episode the show starts to find the balance between funny and poignant. It figures out what it wants to be. I'm in.

It's just hitting Frankie and Grace that their lives aren't at all what they want them to be right now. In an act of midlife rebellion, they decide to go buy some cigarettes to relieve their stress. When they get to the store, they're completely ignored by the employees, who wait on everybody else but them. Grace freaks out, absolutely refusing to be irrelevant. Nothing she tries works, so finally (spoiler alert!) Frankie steals the cigarettes. And they get away with it. Because midlife has made them invisible.

I hear lots of forty-to-forever women bemoaning the fact that they feel invisible. The guys at a construction site look right past them to check out their daughters. The hostess completely ignores two midlife women at the restaurant and seats another party instead. That guy on the plane looks right through you when you sit down next to him. Those two younger women in the locker room just keep gossiping and don't even acknowledge us when we walk in.

Isn't it awesome? We are so not the center of the universe anymore, if ever we were. I think that cloak of invisibility is one of the biggest gifts of midlife.

I can understand that at first blush we might start to feel that we're no longer vital or attractive enough to be noticed. That since we're past procreation age, or getting there, society doesn't need us anymore and so we've been discarded. If we went the kids route, our children don't need us the way they used to either, which can leave us feeling lost until we figure out who we are without all that. If we retire from our day job, we have to figure out who we are without all *that.*

But wow, after all those years of extreme visibility—breeding and being hit on and driving carpools and working crazy hours—the pressure is off, at least a little bit. We don't have to try to be all things to all people. After living our lives as such uber adults, suddenly we don't have to be quite so responsible.

Which is why just about every boomer movie has a pot scene. There's something about the idea of going back to those wild and crazy days, as if the time we've spent being a grownup has just been one long, intense dream. And even if it wasn't a dream, after all that worrying about our kids, how cool would it be to let them worry about us for a change.

Obviously, the idea of our kids bailing us out of jail is much funnier as a fantasy than it would be in reality. There's a scene in my novel *Best Staged Plans* where two midlife women, old friends from high school, fantasize about scoring a joint on the street and smoking it together. A reader sent me a furious email saying that she's always talked up my books to friends and posted reviews online, but she wanted me to know she won't be doing it with *this book*. Because I should be ashamed of myself for advocating drug use, which in case I hadn't noticed is morally and legally wrong.

I don't get many gotcha emails, but when I do I think they're best ignored, so that's what I did. But this woman missed the point. I wasn't advocating smoking marijuana, any more than *Grace and Frankie* was advocating cigarette smoking or shoplifting. It's a metaphor for those good ol' days, back before we were responsible adults and knew better.

And now we're invisible. What I think about invisibility is this: Nobody's looking. Nobody needs us. *Woo-hoo!* Enjoy it while it lasts. Because we're all old enough to know how quickly that other shoe can drop. Lots of midlife women are raising grandchildren. Lots of others are taking care of aging parents or sick spouses or sick friends.

Invisibility is our superpower. Since nobody can see us, we can fly right under the radar. We can get away with doing all the awesome things we want to do.

That Thing

Ella Fitzgerald is singing "It Don't Mean a Thing (If It Ain't Got That Swing)" but I'm hearing it as *It don't mean a thing if we ain't got that thing*. Which is why I'd never make it as a songwriter.

But I digress. What I'm trying to say is that when we're flying around in our invisibility cloaks, looping and gliding aimlessly can get old really fast. So having that thing is key. Something that's so engrossing we get completely lost in it. So lost that we don't even notice that nobody's noticing us. Or if we do happen to notice, we don't give a rat's a*s.

At opposite ends of the spectrum are two forty-to-forever women. One pulls on some baggy sweats and curls up in a recliner clutching the remote. The other plants herself in front of the mirror and freaks out over every new wrinkle, fighting the impossible battle of trying to hang on to her youth, a battle that's only going to get tougher with each passing year. Neither one of them is having much fun.

Because neither one has found her thing. I guess you could argue that watching television and watching for wrinkles can be things, too. But I'm going to go out on a limb here and say I think we all need something better to think about than our next wrinkle. We need something more compelling than the remote.

Our thing has to be more active, more of an adventure. It has to spark our curiosity, challenge us, bring us pleasure, broaden our horizons, keep those neurons firing and making new connections. Our thing has to be something that we wake up every morning, or at least lots of mornings, looking forward to. Our thing has to have something to do with what we want this chapter of our lives to be.

And at midlife, because for so many of us it's been so long, I think our thing should be all about us.

Lots of midlife women I know are doing awesome things for other people—starting charities, serving on boards and committees, running fundraisers, doing meaningful work all over the place. They're doing incredible things for animals. Helping others can give us purpose. It's huge. It's admirable. It can make such an enormous difference to so many.

But lots of these same women have no idea how to give to themselves. It feels too frivolous. Too selfish.

I'm not saying they should give up all that important work. But maybe it's time to take a page from Dr. Seuss and open the door to Thing One and Thing Two.

I was once one of these women.

Embarrassing flashback: I receive a gift certificate as a thank you for something I've done for some group. I've got a little bit of time to kill before I go to work or drive the next carpool or do something else for some other deserving group.

And I figure I might as well spend the gift certificate before I lose it or forget about it—or donate it to yet another deserving group. So I'm wandering around this funky little shop packed with great stuff. And I see all sorts of things to buy for my kids and my husband and a couple of people who have birthdays coming up. But I'm determined, just this once, to buy something for me.

And I can't find a single thing. I mean, I really can't. I

don't know how to buy myself something nonessential anymore. I don't know what I want anymore. I don't know who I am. Finally, I grab something so I can get rid of the stupid gift certificate and I don't have to come back and do this all over again.

I just remembered what I bought that day. A gray soapstone dish with clean modern lines and a little soapstone heart sitting in it. Yikes, that actually gave me goose bumps—probably heart-shaped ones!

It takes me a while, but I finally find both the soapstone dish and the heart—they're buried in the bottom of the box where I found my tap shoes. I make a place for them on the shelf with my heart-shaped rocks.

A couple days ago: I get an email from a midlife woman who heard me speak at a women's conference and has recently finished reading *Never Too Late*. Carol Ann works seven days a week for a local nonprofit. She says it just hit her that she has spent her entire life serving others and always putting herself last.

And now she's finally started doing things for herself. She splurged on a leopard print purse. The following week she got a manicure, not for a work event but just because she felt like it. "My heart does a little happy dance every time I take one of these baby steps," she writes. And she's circling her way back to a book she started writing ages ago and hasn't looked at in years.

If I could pick only one step to help us grow awesome instead of old, if I had to write a haiku instead of a book, it would be this: Find your thing.

Okay, that's not a haiku. So here's my Shine On haiku:

Buried dream seeks light,
Dawn breaks bright in true blue sky.
Fly! Your thing is here.

Maybe I'd never make it as a haiku poet either. But that's okay. I had fun anyway.

If you're feeling a haiku coming on, write it below and/or in your Shine On notebook. (Just to refresh your memory, a haiku is 3 lines and 17 syllables—5 in the first line, 7 in the second, 5 in third.)

____

____

____

About That Thing

The Isley Brothers are singing "It's Your Thing." As they should be.

Even though it took me until I was almost 45 to write my first book, I've known that writing was my thing since I was a little girl. I love being able to play with words all day, tweaking them this way and that, figuring out what I'm trying to say and searching for the best way to say it. My thing is endlessly fascinating to me. I learn and grow with every book I write.

I'm incredibly grateful to be able to support myself as a writer. But even if I couldn't, writing would still be my thing.

I don't think it's the least bit necessary to make a living with our thing. In fact, I think there's a good argument to be made for getting a nice steady paycheck for something else. And doing our thing on the side. I talk about this in *Never Too Late*, but I didn't quit my teaching job until I was sure I could pay my bills with my writing. If I'd quit sooner, I think the pressure would have derailed me. I'm not even sure writing would still be my thing. Expecting my writing to produce enough income to survive on might have sucked the joy right out of it for me.

So many forty-to-forever women I've met have lifelong

buried dreams like I did. If they're really honest with themselves, they already know what their thing is. They just have to work up the courage to dust off their dream and start playing with it again. Having hidden from my own dream for decades, I know how hard that is. But I also know how amazing it feels when you finally go for it.

Maybe you buried your own dream so long ago you can't even remember what it is. Think back. What was that thing you used to love to do before your hormones kicked in and you discovered boys and forgot all about everything else? (Or was that just me?)

If you can't remember your buried dream, so what. Who cares. You can find a new thing.

Or maybe you've simply never found your thing. That's okay, too. Lots of forty-to-forever women haven't. I'd say about half the women (and those few good men!) who attend my reinvention workshops are still looking for their thing. The others know what they want and are trying to figure out how to get there.

Experimenting with new things can be a big part of the fun. After a decade and a half of daily devotion to my writing thing, it's been so enjoyable to shake it up a bit, to step out of my author box, to have some fresh experiences and maybe even find a sub thing or two along the way.

We don't have to be good at our thing. It doesn't have to be serious or impressive. Our thing just needs to make our heart sing.

The Troggs take that as a cue and jump in with a rowdy rendition of "Wild Thing."

Our thing moves us. It makes everything groovy.

Awesome Things

Ali was overweight and had just been diagnosed with hypertension. She was also in therapy recovering from Battered Wife Syndrome. "I was a shell of a woman," she says. "I didn't know who I was anymore. I didn't even feel alive."

One of Ali's friends convinced her to go to a gym with her. A year later, the gym hired a kettlebell teacher. By then Ali had dropped weight and gained confidence, so she jumped right in to the class. Kettlebells turned out to be Ali's thing, and four years later, she began competing. She's now one of the best kettlebell lifters in the country and uses her platform to encourage plus-size women to work out.

Sylvie has purple streaks in her silver hair and a funky tattoo on the inside of her forearm that says *la mer* (the sea). She began working with clay, which she loved. Then she jumped to cake decorating. Now she's making plans to start a cake decorating business. Sylvie is divorced and her two kids are flying on their own. She's ready for a move, and she's narrowed it down to Savannah or Charleston.

Connie's thing is golf. Eileen has rediscovered photography. Wendy has joined a bicycle club. Carol rides with a women's motorcycle club. Jan and Tina have started knitting.

Cindy is taking Italian classes. Lisa just started tap dance lessons. Laura is painting and fishing. Karen began running and quilting. Diane learned to play the guitar. Candy started writing plays and just had one produced.

Maddie has started an Etsy shop to sell vintage items. Sutzi worked in retail at a major department store years ago, but this time around she's launched her own business and is selling in a local marketplace.

Renee started refinishing furniture. "The fact that I now want to spend time at Home Depot wandering around 'just looking' has left my family flabbergasted."

Roxi has found "so many things," including quilting, writing, photography, acrylic painting, woodworking and bead making.

Chris discovered "me time."

Susan is "trying every shiny new thing I can."

Alida loves practicing yoga to music in the early morning hours. Jo is taking a yoga class, which she loves. Alison is taking yoga, too. "And I love love love it!!"

Splish Splash

I'm inspired by these awesome women to try something else at my gym. So I scroll through the schedule and decide to take a water aerobics class.

The first downside I see is that water aerobics requires getting wet. And I'm not sure I have time for that. Because once you get wet, you have to get dry again. And you have to change your clothes. And put on more moisturizer. It's time-consuming, a hassle.

But of course if I'm honest, what I'm dreading even more is the bathing suit part.

I haven't bought a bathing suit in forever. The ancient one I owned no longer fit so I got rid of it during my wardrobe purge. I'm pretty sure I can't get away with wearing my writing pajamas to a water aerobics class, so shopping seems like my only option.

Bathing suit shopping is the worst kind of shopping. I've yet to meet a midlife woman who wouldn't agree that it brings out every inch of our insecurity. But I'm determined to do it anyway, so as soon as I finish my daily pages, I jump in my car.

I don't want this to be a big, elaborate, expensive, stressful deal. I don't want a sales person checking on me in some fancy dressing room, as if she might be able to do something about the way I look. I'm going for anonymity here. I'm going for invisibility. And fingers crossed, I'm hoping to fly in and out of the store fast.

So I head for the closest place that fits the bill: T.J. Maxx. And wouldn't you know, they don't have a single bathing suit with long sleeves, or even ¾-length sleeves. Maybe I should forget about taking water aerobics and become a long-sleeved bathing suit designer instead. I could use power mesh, that stretchy see-through fabric they use for ballroom dancing costumes. The stuff that makes you look naked but much better. I learned a lot about power mesh when I was researching *Wallflower in Bloom*. I probably still even have the notes somewhere. This could be the next Spanx. This could be my new thing.

I realize I'm getting sidetracked. I'm stalling. So I grab every single bathing suit that might possibly be a contender off the rack.

The woman stationed outside the dressing rooms counts my bathing suits. "Good luck," she says. I resist the urge to say, *What do you mean by that?* She hands me a tag with a number on it.

The harsh fluorescent light in my stark white dressing room cubicle makes me think of an interrogation room. I am not going to torture myself.

I peel off everything but my underpants. I try on the first suit. And then the second one. Ugh.

As I reach for the next bathing suit, The Supremes start to sing "Going Down For The Third Time."

"Thanks," I say. And then I remind myself that it's only a freakin' bathing suit. I'm buying it for the pool at the Y, not a sexy beach in the Caribbean or, horror of horrors, a photo shoot.

The third suit is basic black. It's substantial, but not like it has its own zip code or anything. It's seriously spandexed. It's got some shirring for camouflage. But it's also got some sass.

Even in a three-way mirror under this awful fluorescent light, it looks okay on me. Maybe if I tried on the rest of the bathing suits I've brought into the dressing room, I'd find one that looks better. Maybe if I went to another store, I'd find one that looks even better.

But I decide this one is good enough. I'm not going to obsess over this. I'm never going to find the perfect bathing suit. I'm never going to look perfect in a bathing suit. The important thing is that I get to water aerobics before I chicken out.

I've actually taken water aerobics several times over the last few years. I've been fortunate enough to be invited to speak in Austin, Texas at Lake Austin Spa Resort's For the Love of Books program. I took some great classes each time I was there, including water aerobics. Although it's one thing to be walking around this gorgeous cocoon of a resort, wearing your big white bathrobe up to the edge of the pool, only revealing your bathing suit-clad body for the split second between the time you drop the robe on a poolside chair and you slither into the water.

But now I'm at the Y, and the pool I'm about to jump into is a lot more public. A big glass wall exposes it to every single person who walks into the building. I wrap my beach towel around my bathing suit in the locker room. I keep my flip-flops on until I get as close to the pool as I can.

I kick off the flip-flops, hang my towel on a hook, and get in the water as fast as I can. And it's not like I'm comparing my body to the other women's bodies in the pool. Wait, that's a lie. I'm totally doing that. But not a single person in this pool has a perfect body. Or even a perfect bathing suit. No one cares how I look. Except for me.

So I try hard to let it go. It's too exhausting, too boring. I remind myself I've got way more interesting things to think about than how I look in a bathing suit.

The class turns out to be really fun. I love the booming, upbeat music. It's a saltwater pool, which makes me think of the beach. Exercising in the water feels as gentle as womb-walking, yet it sneaks up on you and gives you a surprisingly good workout.

Water aerobics is a non-weight bearing exercise. The water makes our bodies about 90% lighter, which reduces the impact on our joints. It's great for anyone who has arthritis, or foot or back or knee problems. The water provides support for stretching, as well as built-in resistance for strength and cardiovascular conditioning. Water aerobics improves our balance and our core strength.

And once I get over—or at least mostly over—being in a bathing suit, I'm so glad I'm here.

More Awesome Things

Sharon is realizing "I can actually do things I want to do. My favorite is to go out for breakfast accompanied by my Kindle. I eat, enjoy a couple cups of coffee, and spend a wonderful, peaceful hour."

Amy began painting when she lost her job and needed something to do while she was looking for another job. She's still job-hunting, but along the way she's found her thing and is having fun with it.

Lynn has found photography for the first time. "It makes taking a walk an adventure of hunting for that great shot and being very present!"

Ginger loved designing clothing into her 20s "and then life took over." Now she's pulling out her sketchbooks as well as "the many ideas that have been unconsciously stored over those dormant years."

Anne discovered Zumba. "The music is so catchy. Plus I have met a lot of really nice women. In fact, five of us went to Cancun for a week and spent some time beaching it, soaking up some culture, and learning interesting things about ourselves and each other in the process. And no arguments or fights, not once."

Wanda found time to start reading again. Jennifer rediscovered a fantasy series she loved as a child and is rereading and blogging about it.

Kerrin says she discovered herself at midlife. That she finally came to the realization that "trite as it may seem," as long as she is happy with herself, others are happy with her, too. And if not, "then the Gallic shrug of *so what/tant pis/too bad* applies."

Tamela says, "I rediscovered myself, a love for writing, a love for art, and I discovered talents that I did not know I had."

Lisa not only learned to drive for the first time, but she bought a Harley. "That's what happens when both daughters make you a grandma within three months!"

Rebecca says, "My mind has shifted from being all about work to indulging my creative side. I am putting more time into my sewing, crocheting, knitting, and gardening. I crave the sense of peace and calm that comes with my hobbies."

As Goethe said, "As soon as you trust yourself, you will know how to live."

So Over It

"I'm tired of playing worn-out depressing ladies in frayed bathrobes," Joanne Woodward said. "I'm going to get a new hairdo and look terrific and go back to school and even if nobody notices, I'm going to be the most self-fulfilled lady on the block."

There are only so many hours in a day. Letting go of the things we're over can free up time for more awesome things and allow us to say yes to ourselves.

Barb is over "worrying about imaginary scenarios" and how she's going to handle them when and if they ever happen.

Cindy is over caring about material things like she used to. "If it breaks, it breaks."

Rebecca is over weighing herself every day and "letting the number dictate whether I like myself or hate myself that day."

Angie has "let go of the drama and stopped worrying about what others are doing in their lives."

Pat has stopped collecting friends "as if there's some kind of prize for whoever has the most. How many friends do you really need?"

Brenda is over "the needy people in my life who always want something and never have anything to give."

Me, I know I'm over dyeing my hair. I know I'm over owning lots of stuff.

And at midlife, I know I'm seriously over entertaining.

I flash back to when our kids were little, and Jake and I, exhausted from the week, would spend an entire Saturday cooking and cleaning for company that evening. We'd plop the kids down in front of the TV for a marathon of *Care Bears* and *Ghostbusters*. We'd work our butts off. We'd snap at each other. We'd ignore our kids.

There's no point in looking back, in saying that if I had to do it all over again, I'd forget about entertaining and spend the entire day making a great big creative mess with my kids. Because—who knew—in a blink that precious time with them would be over. But there is absolutely a point in not doing the entertaining thing anymore if I don't want to do it. Because I'm old enough to know that in a blink this precious time will be over, too.

There are forty-to-forever women who love to entertain, who love to cook. Unbelievable as it seems to me, I've even heard that there are midlife women out there who actually take pleasure in cleaning.

I'm not one of them. I hate cleaning. I don't enjoy cooking either. I don't really like sitting around at a table, even at a restaurant. I spend way too much time sitting at my computer, so I much prefer to save the chatting for something like a nice long walk.

But I really suck at saying no. And while I like to think I've come a long way, apparently I haven't completely gotten over the disease to please. Instead of just announcing that I don't entertain anymore, I sometimes let myself get nudged into extending a vague invitation to host "when things slow down." Though I know full well my life hasn't slowed down once in the last decade and a half. And even if it did, this isn't the thing I'd choose to do with the extra time.

Sometimes it feels easier to just go along. We don't want the confrontation. We don't want to hurt the other person's feelings. But by putting what this person wants over what we want, we're not choosing the life we desire. Plus we have to clean our house.

If a friend wants to do A and I hate A, I don't have to do it. If I want to do B and she hates B, then she doesn't have to do that. We can find a C we both like to do together. And we can do A and B with other friends, like back in the day when we knew which of our friends we could count on to play Barbie or Red Rover.

As my Facebook friend Melissa said, "I've discovered that I can say no without guilt."

Learning how to say no in a positive way is key. *I'm spending as much time as I can enjoying nature/trying new things/staying off my butt these days,* I vow to say the next time. *So I don't entertain anymore. But let me know if you want to go for a bike ride!*

Nobody's perfect. We're all flawed and we do the best we can given what we have to work with. But if a friend just keeps pushing us to do the things we don't want to do, maybe that friendship has run its course. Sometimes we outgrow our friendships and we've got to let go of a friend or two to make room for other, more supportive friends. We can have compassion for someone and still choose to spend our time with friends who lift us up rather than bring us down.

It can be harder to make new friends at midlife, but it's worth the effort. The experts say we should put ourselves in situations where we'll find like-minded people—a meetup.com photography group, a book club at the library, a continuing education class. A friend of mine once took a part-time job as an usher at a local theater. She got a bird's eye view of the performances, which she loved, and she eventually even ended up with a walk-on part in a play. Best of all, she made some new friends.

The experts also say that once we put ourselves in new situations, we have to push ourselves to strike up conversations. Every once in a while we'll connect with a kindred spirit who's looking for a friend, too.

"Find a group of people who will challenge and inspire you, spend a lot of time with them, and it will change your life," Amy Poehler said.

Healthy friendships are a two-way street, balanced and reciprocal, with each friend helping and supporting the other through good times and bad. Healthy friendships feel good to both friends. They help us grow. They change to accommodate each person's individual growth. These friends don't consistently try to manipulate us into doing things we don't want to do. Healthy friendships make us feel good, not drained or used, after we've spent time with this person.

I feel a list coming on.

Things I'm Over

1. Entertaining
2. One-way friendships
3. Drama
4. Sitting
5. Saying yes when I want to say no

Your turn:

Things I'm Over

1.
2.

3.
4.
5.

Birds of a Feather

So the cats and I are looking for a little fun.

Julie Andrews breaks into "Feed the Birds" from *Mary Poppins*. Okay then, we'll take Mary Poppins' advice. We'll feed the little birds and show them we care.

I don't want to risk being lured away from my computer to bird watch before I've finished writing my daily pages, so I decide to create Birdsville right outside my office window.

One length of my corner desk stretches under the window, and the cats already have desktop beds there. One bed is small, red with white polka dots. The other bed is larger, animal print in shades of brown. The three cats take turns sharing a bed and lounging solo, but the two who share always squish together in the smaller bed, while the other cat enjoys twice as much room as it needs in the bigger bed.

I don't think this means my cats aren't very bright. Instead, I think there's a message here for me: when you want to connect, then get in there and connect, and when you need your space, don't be afraid to stretch out and claim it.

The moment I finish typing that, Pebbles, who has been sharing the smaller bed with Squiggy, stands up and stretches. Then she saunters over to curl up in the bigger bed with

Sunshine, which never happens. Cats don't like to be pigeonholed.

Anyway, whatever their configuration, my cats spend hours and hours hanging out on those beds, napping in warm waves of sunlight, checking out the occasional chipmunk as it dances across the yard. But there's not a lot of action outside that window, so my hope is that Birdsville will make their lives more interesting. And mine, too.

My first thought is to poke a shepherd's hook plant hanger into the ground outside my office window and hang a single bird feeder from it. But then I start browsing online and discover something called the Yard Butler, which holds multiple bird feeders. I mean, why hang one bird feeder when you can hang five? (Perhaps I'm not as over having stuff as I thought I was.)

So I do my research and place my order. I've already got two bird feeders I don't use out in the garage where they're not doing anybody any good, so I can fill them both with black oil sunflower seed, which attracts the widest variety of birds.

I order a hummingbird feeder, because I really love hummingbirds. I make my own hummingbird nectar by mixing one part sugar to four parts water. You just boil the water for three minutes, then add the sugar and stir. When it cools, fill the feeder and store the rest in the fridge until you need it. Change the nectar every three days or so, especially in warm months, before it starts to get cloudy.

Don't add red food coloring, which some pre-made hummingbird food contains, since food coloring isn't any better for hummingbirds than it is for humans. The red color of the hummingbird feeder is all they need to find it.

These are the things I worry about, so it's good to find out that we can't prevent hummingbirds from migrating south when they should be by leaving our hummingbird feeder out year round. The most significant trigger for bird migration is the shortening in the length of the days, not lack of food.

I order a tall finch feeder with multiple feeding ports and some nyjer seed because I'm hoping to attract goldfinches for their tropical yellow color and their cheery song. And also because finches like to travel and feed together in groups, and a group of finches is called a charm. I just love that, and I really want to be able to say, *Look, a charm of goldfinches!*

I also decide to plant a bird garden down the road—yellow sunflowers and pink coneflowers and black-eyed Susans.

So everything arrives and eventually Birdsville is all set up. The cats and I keep our eyes peeled for a shimmer of hummingbirds, a scold of bluejays, a quarrel of sparrows, a chime of wrens, a descent of woodpeckers. Anything, really.

The birds are a total no-show. But before long Birdsville is discovered by the chipmunks. Chipmunk after chipmunk scampers up the long center pole of the Yard Butler and fills its cheeks with black sunflower seeds. I watch, hoping the chipmunks will slide back down like it's a fire pole, but instead they turn and scurry down headfirst and zigzag away.

The cats are enthralled. They're in chipmunk heaven. It's as if they're watching cat TV and they've just discovered they have free unlimited access to reruns of *Chip 'n' Dale.*

But I really wanted birds. So I'm thinking I should try to find a way to redirect the chipmunks, preferably to someone else's yard, in case they're keeping the birds away.

My son Kaden, who I can always count on for fresh perspective, stops by my office to check out Birdsville. I bring him up to speed.

"If the point is to entertain the cats," he says, "why does it matter whether they're chipmunks or birds?"

This is a really good point. But I order the squirrel baffle anyway, because no matter how the cats feel, *I'd* like to be entertained by birds. Once the baffle, which looks like one of those cones that dogs have to wear around their necks so they don't eat their stitches, is wrapped around the Yard Butler, the chipmunks can only access a seed-filled saucer beneath it.

And the birds finally show. First chickadees and then house wrens. And one day a hummingbird makes its way over to the feeder after stopping first at a bright red star-shaped flower on a nearby Cypress vine. A week after that, the goldfinches arrive in all their glory to feed on nyjer seed.

And I finally get to say it: *Oh, look, a charm of goldfinches!*

Bird watching is a great way to relax and unwind, and a truly fabulous way to procrastinate when you're supposed to be writing your daily pages. It makes us feel close to nature. It's hard to obsess about the little things when you're watching birds.

There are people who say we shouldn't be feeding the birds at all, but I've done the reading, and especially given extreme weather and dwindling natural habitats, I'm good with it. But you might want to do some Googling and make your own decision.

"I hope you love birds too," Emily Dickinson wrote. "It is economical. It saves going to heaven."

If you decide to start watching the birds, you can take part in the next The Great Backyard Bird Count. More than 100,000 people of all ages participate in this four-day count each February to "create an annual snapshot of the distribution and abundance of birds." You can even win prizes—bird feeders, of course! There's also a photography contest, with some amazing entries from all over the world. Go to www.gbbc.birdcount.org to find out more.

I'm definitely in. The cats are still thinking about it.

Even More Awesome Things

Elizabeth rediscovered her art at midlife. On a dare from a photographer friend, she agreed to draw every day with this friend for 30 days. Five years later, Elizabeth is working as an artist. She's been in shows, she's sold her work, and she's been commissioned to create art for clients.

Moira started cycling. She hadn't been on a bike in 25 years. She didn't even know how to shift. And now she's finished 100-mile rides. "It astounds me. I've gotten so much from it—who knew!"

Barbara also starting biking. And she discovered "the joy and freedom of riding a bike." As did Debbi, who now participates in weeklong bike tours.

Bike riding is Lori's thing, too. "It's just as fun as when I was 10. And I'm pretty sure it's the closest we can get to flying without wings."

Lisa has been doing lots of rediscovering. She landed a position as a community columnist, wrote a novel, took up photography again.

Marie rediscovered her love of music. She learned to play the ukulele and took up the piano again, which she began playing the first time around at 5.

Kristen is rediscovering exercise "after sitting on the couch for a number of years." She's also "hoping to rediscover my toes!"

Paula has discovered gardening and canning. She says they calm and relax her, get her outside, give her exercise. Stacy has discovered gardening and canning, too.

Karen got a puppy, which "brought much needed excitement to my life." Cindi got "my first puppy that is all my own. She is amazing!" Phyllis adopted an older dog from a shelter and says "he's just the sweetest thing and gets me out walking twice a day."

Timia is fostering kittens. "And getting rid of all the stuff accumulated during a long marriage that has ended."

Kim rescues cats. After a particularly stressful day at work, "I found myself wishing I could be holding a purring kitten because it is so calming."

Terry rediscovered meditation, and relearned that "it really does make my day go more smoothly, as long as I do it, and not just think about doing it. Now, if I can just remember that every day!"

Brenda always wanted to play the piano, and now she's in her second year of lessons.

Sandy has started a writing/education blog and self-published a booklet about teaching.

Bernie discovered writing and bird watching.

Honey discovered that Facebook is a wonderful tool to reunite old friends, and it played an important part in organizing a recent high school class reunion.

Susan's midlife thing is boating—power and sailing, and now cruising. "It's a great way to explore so much beauty in the world and in our own neighborhoods."

Angie says her new thing is simplicity. "Life doesn't have to be complicated and difficult. You just have to let go of the drama and not worry about what others are doing in their lives."

Kathleen's thing is listening to classical music. "Ahhh. Soothes the soul."

Loretta discovered she could sing jazz and has since made a jazz album.

Linda finally quit the job she'd hated for years. She now works part-time at a stress-free job that she enjoys, and which frees up time to find her thing.

Tina started camping at midlife, "and I absolutely love the peace and tranquility it brings." A friend has also introduced Tina to photography.

Bev and Katherine have both discovered line dancing.

Barb and Claire and Rosemary have found knitting.

Carol has rediscovered quilting. "I loved quilting in my 20s, but as my professional life became more demanding, my creative side languished. Now retired, I am having a wonderful and fulfilling time quilting and sewing again."

Garnet started painting. "And I don't mean redecorating," she adds.

Dawn began coaching high school football. "Best time ever."

Color My World

Rebecca's new thing is coloring. "I love coloring books! I have a whole collection of my own pencils and crayons!"

Lisa loves coloring in "grown-up coloring books with intricate patterns."

Denise's nephew gave her a coloring book for her 50th birthday. "I love coloring with my pencils!"

Dee and Cyndi have started coloring, too.

These forty-to-forever women have lots of company. Coloring has become a midlife thing.

The repetitive, gentle motions of coloring help relieve our stress and anxiety. Coloring helps rekindle our creativity. It puts something in our hand besides a potato chip. Coloring triggers childhood memories and reminds us of simpler times.

I haven't colored since my kids were kids, so I head for the store and grab some colored pencils and crayons. I spend a long time flipping through coloring books for adults, which are everywhere these days.

There are plenty of great coloring books to choose from, but I can't seem to decide. I finally realize that what I really want to do is try to create my own. Maybe not a whole coloring book, but at least a coloring page or two.

I have no problem at all picturing these potential coloring pages in full detail. I'm ready to jump right in. Until I remember that I don't have the skills to draw the coloring pages I envision. Bummer. Maybe I should have learned to draw horses back in elementary school after all. But I'm definitely not up for putting in the time to do it now.

I ponder this for a while, trying to come up with a creative solution. I decide to see if I can convert some of the photographs I've taken into coloring pages. If it works, it will bypass the drawing thing completely. And if it doesn't work, oh well.

I love taking photographs. I love the way it trains my eyes to see details I'd otherwise miss. I love how the camera captures things I hadn't even noticed until I looked at the photo. I love the way photographs preserve special moments, and ordinary moments, too. The only thing I hate is that whenever I carry my camera with me on a walk or start taking photos with my phone, I never get a decent workout in because I stop every three seconds to take another picture.

I've got plenty of photos. I choose one I took of a huge goddess topiary at the Atlanta Botanical Gardens. I do a little bit of Googling on how to make coloring pages, and then I open the photo in Photoshop Elements. I check to make sure the foreground is black. I click on Filter, and then Sketch, and then Photocopy. I play around to get as much contrast as I can.

And it works pretty well! I would totally color this page!

If you want to try doing this and you don't have Photoshop Elements or another photo editor with a Photocopy setting, you can find lots of online tutorials on how to make your own coloring pages from photographs with free online editors like pixlr.com.

I turn some more photos into coloring pages—a vase filled with hydrangeas, shells on a beach. I'm inspired. I'm having fun. And I haven't even started coloring yet.

I read that coloring can become a kind of meditation, especially if you color a mandala. Mandalas are complex and symmetrical circular geometric designs that have long been used to trigger meditation. The idea is that the design pulls us in and quiets our mind, which is soothing and allows our creativity to emerge.

The mandala is one of the most ancient art forms. The word *mandala* is Sanscrit for *circle*, and mandalas can be found in many religions. Even in nature. The snowflake is a perfect mandala.

When we draw a mandala, it's supposed to be a reflection of who we are and how we're feeling.

"A mandala is the psychological expression of the totality of the self," Jung said.

Drawing a mandala a day in our Shine On notebook might be an interesting way to journal, maybe even more interesting than wine cork journaling.

But first I've got to figure out how to draw one. And so I Google up some mandala tutorials. I create a square, make a dot in the exact center of the square, make a series of ever-widening circles with a compass, add some X shapes through the whole thing to create a circular grid.

Then I repeat a simple shape over and over again in each section around the circle. I try to take my time, trusting that the mandala will take on depth and intricacy with the repetition of each new shape I add.

In no time at all, my mandala is a hot mess. If this is a reflection of the totality of my self, I am so screwed.

Okay, so I can't draw horses *or* mandalas.

But in an effort to redeem myself, I find this great free site, colormandala.com, which allows me to create the mandalas of my dreams. I spend far too much time there, creating mandala after mandala. After I finish each one, I go to Actions>Download at the top of the screen and save them to my computer.

Then I print them out and spend some happy hours coloring my own creations.

Because sharing makes everything more fun, I decide to make a free Shine On coloring book and give it away. Go to http://ClaireCook.com/coloring-book/ to download yours.

Enjoy!

Winging It

So the Fifth Dimension are singing "Up, Up and Away."

"Great Girlfriend Getaways," Jill, the heroine of my novel *Seven Year Switch*, answers the phone when she's working. "Feisty and fabulous man-free escapes both close to home and all over the world. When was the last time you got together with *your* girlfriends?"

Midlife women are traveling like never before. We're traveling for adventure. We're traveling for cultural immersion. We're traveling for growth and renewal. We're traveling to learn, to play, to have some fun. We're traveling to spend time with old friends, to connect with new like-minded friends. We're using our money to accumulate experiences and memories instead of things.

Sharon is going to Tanzania on safari. Amy went to England, Wales, and Ireland. Cindy took a cooking class in Tuscany. Cheryl traveled to the island of Capri. Pamela went on a cruise to Alaska.

Pam discovered Cape Cod—"something about this beautiful place touches my soul." Laura studied French in a total immersion program in the south of France. Carol just left to travel through Australia, New Zealand, and Fiji.

Reilly and Mary want to travel the world. Janet wants to go coasteering in Ireland. Karen wants to see Thailand. Jane has her sights set on Costa Rica. Lee wants to go to the Galapagos Islands. Cindy wants to go to China. Janice wants to try rafting on the Colorado River through the Grand Canyon. Jen wants to go to Greece. Linda wants to visit every state in the United States. Beth would love to make a tour of all the vineyards in the world.

While many midlife women travel with spouses and partners, more and more of them are traveling with friends. Sometimes these women are single or divorced or widowed. Sometimes the issue is that stick-in-the-mud husband who doesn't want to go anywhere. Sometimes the reason is money —when only half of a couple travels, and the other person doesn't really want to go anyway, it cuts costs in half. And sometimes it's just fun to have an adventure with a friend you don't get to spend time with very often.

Viking River Cruises told me they're seeing an increase in friends traveling together on their cruises, and the fact that their beds easily convert from a king size to two twin beds makes it easy to share a stateroom.

Great Girlfriend Getaways in *Seven Year Switch* might be a figment of my imagination, but there are lots of real women-only travel groups out there, including Adventure Women, Gutsy Women Travel, Senior Women Travel (50+), Journeys of Discovery, Women Traveling Together.

If you don't have a travel buddy, no worries. These groups will give you the support and company you're looking for. They can also pair you with a roommate.

Over the course of my midlife author gig, I've traveled alone quite a bit. It's taught me that I can navigate any airport if I just follow the signs for the baggage claim. And that there are kind people everywhere who will be happy to help me out if I ask nicely.

Jake is great to travel with, and I love traveling with friends as well. But if I travel with someone else, we tend to stay in our own little bubble. When I travel alone, I'm forced out of my comfort zone, where the growth always happens. I connect more, make more friends. And it's really empowering.

One of my favorite solo trips was to give the keynote at We Move Forward, a fabulous women's conference on gorgeous Isla Mujeres (Island of Women), Mexico. I talk about it more in *Never Too Late*, but if you're looking for a group of warm and welcoming women you'd feel comfortable joining by yourself, I can't recommend it enough. It would also be a great trip to take with friends. (wemoveforward.com)

My friend Barbara Weibel takes solo travel to another level. She quit her job and hit the road, and has been traveling solo full time for almost nine years now! Visit Hole in the Donut Cultural Travel to see what Barbara's up to and to get some great travel trips. (holeinthedonut.com)

Another free travel resource for women you should know about is journeywoman.com, which offers things like insights into the customs and taboos of travel destinations around the world, as well as What to Wear, Where, which is a country-by-country what-to-wear database. Another resource is hermail.net, a free service that allows women to connect with other women travelers anywhere in the world—a great way to get insider advice for a trip you're about to take.

When money is an issue, lots of women are getting creative. Angie "stopped buying lattes, started packing a lunch for work, and decided I didn't need that new car after all. I'd much rather travel."

Julia downsized to a smaller place. "Our expenses are about half what they were, which means more trips."

And there's always that senior discount fund!

You might try pitching a class you're qualified to teach to a tour group. Many cruise lines use guest lecturers as well as instructors—they're rarely paying gigs, but your cruise and airfare are covered. Even though you pay to be part of an expedition with Earthwatch Institute, the contribution is tax deductible. Travel bloggers who build big followings get offered hosted, aka free, trips just so they'll write about them.

Kate has done several home exchanges to make travel more affordable. Denise bought an old RV. Donna is working hard to pay down her debt, "but every once in a while I grab a friend and hit the road. You don't have to go far to have fun!"

Traveling gives us a sense of freedom. It strips away our familiar routines and helps us get in touch with who we are underneath all that. Travel boosts our creativity. Our brain has to make new connections as we problem solve in unfamiliar situations. Travel opens our eyes and minds and hearts to new ways of living and thinking.

"Never lose an opportunity of seeing anything that is beautiful," Emerson wrote. "Welcome it in every face, in every skip, in every flower."

As soon as I realize I'm perfectly content just hanging around being creative and trying new things, I'm ready to plan a trip. I glance up at my wine cork vision board. The picture of those rolling fields of lavender calls out to me, and in an instant I know I'm heading for Provence. I don't know when and I don't know how yet. I only know I'm going. The lavender will be in bloom, and I'll write another adventure for the women in *The Wildwater Walking Club*.

I commit to it. I write it in my Shine On notebook.

Your turn.

What's your next trip?

Shiny Night Candlelight

It comes to me in the middle of the night that I'd like to start a new tradition called Shiny Night Candlelight. I have no idea what it is yet, especially since I'm mostly asleep, but clearly it involves candles, so that's where I'll start.

The next day I find two beeswax candles in a drawer. I love their warm glow, their honey-tinged smell. But I want more.

So I decide to make my own beeswax candles. I Google up a few tutorials. I order two 8-by-16-inch sheets of beeswax plus wicking online for under $15.

When my candle-making supplies arrive, I cut one of the beeswax sheets in half so I have two 4-by-16-inch sheets. I fold each one in half the other way so I have four 4-by-8-inch sheets, and fold them in half again so I have eight 4-by-4-inch sheets. When my math headache subsides, I cut the folded lines with scissors and separate my eight beeswax pieces.

I cut 5-inch pieces of wicking so that I can expose an inch of the wick on one end for lighting. Then I just lay the wick close to one edge of a square of beeswax. I bend over a tiny bit of wax and press down firmly from one end to the other to hold the wick in place.

Then I roll the candle, gently so that I don't mess up the beautiful honeycomb pattern. When I get to the end, I carefully press it into the rest of the candle to seal it.

In practically no time, I've finished making the candles. Easy breezy. You don't even have to melt the wax.

Shiny Night Candlelight turns out to be a simple, peaceful tradition. Lights out except for the flickering glow of my beeswax candles. Soft music. It's calming. It's restorative.

"There are two ways of spreading light: to be the candle or the mirror that reflects it," Edith Wharton wrote.

I'm not sure if I'm shining or reflecting the light, but maybe if we're lucky, we get to do a little bit of both in our lives.

It hits me that Shiny Night Candlelight might be a birthday celebration. I started this book with a milestone birthday on the horizon, and now I've sailed past it and come full circle.

This is the year I turned 60. I'm 60. 60! How can that be?

When I was 20, I thought that any life even remotely worth living would be long over at 40. 60 didn't even factor into my consciousness. How bizarre to still feel 20 in some ways. How strange to find out that, for better or worse, I'm still me after all these years.

If I'm fortunate enough to hit 80 or 90 or even triple digits, I hope I'll look up from the book I'm writing then, or from whatever my new thing is, and laugh about what a kid I was at 60. And then I'll lace up my sneakers and head out for a long walk.

Sixty. 60. It's a number that means nothing. It's a number to rock proudly. A number to be transcended and reinvented. And ultimately a number to let go of—there are so many more interesting things to think about.

Maybe Shiny Night Candlelight isn't a birthday celebration after all. Maybe it's really an unbirthday celebration, not just for me, but for all of us. And so, like the March Hare in *Alice in Wonderland*, I wish us all a very merry unbirthday.

Because maybe that's what we should be celebrating, not that milestone birthday, or the single day every year when that number gets shockingly bigger. Maybe we should be celebrating those other amazing and challenging and happy and sad and surprising and beautiful 364 days a year for as long as they keep coming.

I close my eyes and wish us awesomeness with all my heart.

Then I blow out my beeswax candles one by one.

Shine on!

Note from Claire

Thank you so much for reading *Shine On: How to Grow Awesome Instead of Old!*

This book was intended to help and encourage you on your own journey. If it did, I'd be so grateful if you would leave a short review to help other 40-to-forever women find *Shine On*.

I really appreciate your help spreading the word!

Keep turning the virtual pages to read an excerpt of *The Wildwater Walking Club*.

xxxxxClaire

My Gift To You

Don't forget to download your free Shine On coloring book at ClaireCook.com/coloring-book/.

Happy coloring!

The Wildwater Walking Club

DAY 1
132 steps

On the day I became redundant, I began to walk. Okay, not right away. First I lay in bed and savored the sound of the alarm not going off. I'd been hearing that stupid beep at the same ridiculous time pretty much every weekday morning for the entire eighteen years I'd worked at Balancing Act Shoes.

I stretched decadently and let out a loud, self-indulgent sigh. I pictured the zillion-count Egyptian cotton sheets I'd finally get around to buying. I'd pull them up to my chin to create a cozy cocoon, then wiggle down into the feather bed I'd buy, too, a big, fluffy one made with feathers from wildly exotic free-range birds.

I'd once had a pair of peacock earrings that came with a note saying, "Since peacocks lose their feathers naturally, no peacocks were harmed in the making of these earrings." I'd always meant to look that up to see if it was a marketing ploy or if it was actually true. If so, then maybe I could find a peacock feather comforter. Though I suppose what would be the point of using peacock feathers in a comforter if you couldn't see them? Perhaps I could invent a see-through comforter that let the iridescent blues and greens shimmer through. Though I guess first I'd need to come up with a zillion-count see-through Egyptian cotton.

I closed my eyes. I flipped over onto my back and opened them again. I stared up at a serious crack, which I liked to think of as the Mason-Dixon Line of my ceiling. My seventh-grade history teacher would be proud she'd made that one stick.

I rolled over, then back again. I kicked off my ordinary covers. On the first morning I could finally sleep in, I seemed to be more awake than I'd been at this hour in decades. Go figure.

After a long, leisurely shower, a bowl of cereal, and an online check of the news and weather, I called Michael on his cell at 8:45 A.M. It rang twice, then cut off abruptly without going to voice mail.

So I sent him an email. "Call me when you can," it said.

A nanosecond later my email bounced back: "Returned Mail: Permanent Fatal Errors."

I dialed his office number. At least that voice mail picked up. "Hi, it's me," I said. "I seem to be having technical difficulties reaching you. But the good news is I have all the time in the world now. Anyway, call me when you get this." I laughed what I hoped was the perfect laugh, light and sexy. "Unless, of course, you're trying to get rid of me."

By 11 A.M., I'd watched enough morning TV to last me a lifetime, and I still hadn't heard back from him. I tried to remember if we had specific plans for that night. Michael worked for the buyout company, Olympus, so we'd had to keep things on the down low. I mean, it wasn't that big a deal. I was leaving anyway, and he'd be right behind me, so it was just a matter of time.

After the initial army of auditors had stopped acting like nothing was going on, when everybody with half a brain knew something was obviously up at Balancing Act, Michael had been one of the first Olympus managers to come aboard. He was handsome, but not too, and exactly my age, which gave us an immediate bond in an industry that more and more was comprised of iPod-wearing recent college grads. Some of them had become friends, at least work friends, but they were still essentially children.

Michael and I had commonality, both current and past. I was a Senior Manager of Brand Identity for Balancing Act. He was a Senior Brand Communications Manager for Olympus. Potato, potahto. The athletic shoe industry is market-driven rather than product-driven, which means, basically, that even though we don't actually need a two-hundred-dollar pair of sneakers, we can be convinced that we do. Fads can be created, predicted, or at least quickly reacted to, and in a nutshell, that's how Michael and I both spent our days.

But even more important, we'd both danced to Van Morrison's "Moondance," gotten high to the Eagles' "Witchy Woman," made love to "Sweet Baby James" back when James Taylor had hair. Maybe not with each other, but still, we had the generational connection of parallel experiences, coupled with your basic boomer's urge to do something new, fast, while there was still time.

One of the first things he said to me was, "It's business, baby."

We were sitting in the employee cafeteria, and I felt a little jolt when he called me *baby*. He had rich chocolate eyes and a full head of shiny brown hair without a strand of gray, which meant he probably dyed it, but who was I to talk.

"Of course, it's business," I said. I gave my own recently camouflaged hair a little flip and added, "Baby."

He laughed. He had gorgeous white teeth, probably veneers, but so what.

"What's your off-the-record recommendation?" I asked.

He leaned forward over the button-shaped table that separated us, and the arms of his suit jacket gripped his biceps. I caught the sharp, spicy smell of his cologne. Some kind of citrus and maybe a hint of sandalwood, but also something retro. Patchouli?

"The first deal," he said, "is always the best."

"So grab the VRIF and run?" I asked, partly to show off my new vocabulary. Balancing Act employees, even senior managers like me, didn't find out we'd become the latest Olympus acquisition until the day it went public. Since then, the buzz had been that the way to go was to take your package during the VRIF or Voluntary Reductions in Force phase. Olympus was all about looking for redundancies and establishing synergies, code for getting rid of the departments that overlapped.

Right now, the packages were pretty generous. I could coast along for eighteen months at full base salary, plus medical and dental. They were even throwing in outplacement services to help me figure out what to do with the rest of my life. The only thing missing was a grief counselor. And maybe a good masseuse. By the time we got to the Involuntary Reductions in Force phase, aka the IRIF, who knew what I'd be looking at.

Michael glanced over his shoulder, then back into my eyes. "Here's the thing, Noreen. Or do you prefer Nora?"

"Nora," I said, even though no one had ever called me that until this very moment. I'd been called Nor, Norry, Reeny, Beany, NoreanyBeany, even String-Beany, though I had to admit that one was a few years and pounds ago. Mostly it was just plain Noreen. Michael's *baby* reeled me in, but I swallowed his *Nora* hook, line, and sinker.

I forced myself to focus. "Wall Street," he was saying, "will expect some performance from the synergy created by combining companies. The way to get performance is to streamline numbers, to create efficiencies. Human resources, finance, operations, marketing—lots of overlap. Ergo . . ."

I raised my eyebrows. "Ergo?" I teased.

He raised his eyebrows to match mine, and even though it would be another two weeks before we ended up in bed together, I think we both knew right then it was only a matter of time.

I leaned my elbows on the table. "So, what?" I said. "I leave so you can have my job?"

"Off the record," he said, "I'll probably be right behind you. I mean, take my job, please. You'd be doing me a favor. I'm just waiting till they offer the VRIF package to the Olympus employees they've brought in."

"Seriously?" I said. "You really think you'll take it? And do what?"

He laced his fingers together behind his head and arched back in his chair. "Let's see. First off, I think I'd light a bonfire and burn up all my suits and ties. Then I'd chill for a while. Maybe buy a van, find me a good woman, drive cross-country." He smiled. "Then look around for a partner, someone to start a small business with."

At eleven-thirty, I called Michael's cell again. The second ring cut off midway, once more without going to voice mail. I waited, then pushed Redial. This time it cut off almost as soon as it started ringing. I sent another email. It bounced back with the same fatal message. I called his office number, but when that voice mail picked up, I just hung up.

I was seriously creeped out by now. I thought about calling someone else at work to see if maybe there was a logical explanation, like everybody in the whole building was having both cell service and mail server problems, but I couldn't seem to make myself do it.

I thought some more, then threw on a pair of slimming black pants and a coral V-neck top over a lightly padded, modified pushup bra pitched as a cutting-edge scientific undergarment breakthrough in subtle enhancement. A little figure-flattering never hurt, even if it was hyperbole, and if nothing else, the coral worked well with my pale skin and dark hair. The last time I'd worn it, Michael had said I looked hot. Smoking hot, come to think of it, though that was probably an overstatement, too.

The midday drive into Boston was a lot shorter without the commuter congestion. Who knew that unemployment would be the best way to beat the traffic? Still, I had plenty of time to get a plan. I'd simply pretend I'd left one of my favorite sweaters behind and wanted to grab it before someone ran off with it. And I was in the neighborhood anyway because I was meeting a friend for lunch. And I just thought I'd poke my head in and say Hi, Michael. And he'd say he was just thinking about me, trying to remember if we had plans for dinner. I'd tilt my head and tell him if he was lucky, maybe I'd even consider cooking for him. And he'd smile and make a crack about maybe it would be safer to get takeout.

The main lot was packed, but eventually I found a parking spot. I reached into my glove compartment for the lanyard that held my employee badge, slipped it over my head, and made for the front entrance.

When the revolving door spilled me out into the lobby, I held up my badge for the uniformed guard.

He waved his handheld scanner over the laminated bar code like a wand.

I headed for the elevators, the way I had a million times before.

"Ma'am?" he said.

I turned. He held up his scanner. I held out my badge again.

This time I watched. When the laser light hit the bar code, it flashed red instead of the customary green.

We looked at each other. This was the grouchy guard, the one who never said a word and always looked like he wished he were anywhere but here. I found myself wishing I'd tried a little harder to befriend him.

I laughed. "Well, I guess it didn't take them long to get over me." I gave my hair a toss. "Lucky me, I took a buyout. I just need a minute to run up and grab something I forgot." He didn't say anything, so I added, "A sweater. A cardigan. Black, with some nice seaming around the buttons. I'll be back before you even start to miss me."

"Sorry, ma'am, I can't let you do that. Orders."

I blew out a gust of air. "Just call up," I said. "Sixth floor." I held out my card again so he could read my name.

He ran his finger down a list on a clipboard. "Sorry, ma'am. You're on the No Admittance List."

"You're not serious," I said, though it was pretty obvious that he was.

I waited. He looked up again. I met his eyes and couldn't find even a trace of sympathy in them, so I tried to look extra pathetic, which by that point I didn't really even have to fake.

"Maybe you can call somebody and ask them to bring it down," he said finally. "On your cell phone," he added.

"Unbelievable," I said. I stomped across the lobby so I could have some privacy. Since I hadn't really left a sweater behind, I decided to just cut to the chase and call Michael's cell. Half a ring and it went dead.

There is always that exact moment when the last shreds of denial slip away and your reality check bounces. I closed my eyes. Eventually, I opened them again. I called his office number. "You piece of shit," I whispered to his voice mail.

I stood there for a minute, scratching my scalp with both

hands. Hard, as if I might somehow dig my way to a good idea. When that didn't happen, I walked out, without even a glance at the guard. I kept my head up high as I walked across the parking lot, in case some-one was watching from one of the windows. I found my car and climbed back into it.

Just as I was getting ready to pull out onto the ac-cess road, I caught the purple-and-white-striped Balancing Act Employee Store awning out of the corner of my eye. I banged a right and pulled into a parking space right in front of it.

I stopped at the first circular display I came to and grabbed a pair of our, I mean *their*, newest shoe, the Walk On By, in a size 8½. It was strictly a women's model, positioned as the shoe every woman needed to walk herself away from the things that were holding her back and toward the next exciting phase of her life. *Shed the Outgrown. Embrace Your Next Horizon. Walk On By.*

Even though I'd been part of the team to fabricate this hook out of thin air, I still wanted to believe in the possibility. I handed the box to the woman at the register. I held up my badge. I held my breath.

Her scanner flashed green, and she rattled off a price that was a full 50 percent off retail.

"Wait," I said. I ran back to the display, grabbing all the Walk On Bys in my size. Then I sprinted around the room, scooping up whatever I could find in an 8½. Dream Walker. *(You'll Swear You're Walking on Clouds.)* Step Litely. *(Do These Sneakers Make Me Look Thin?)* Feng Shuoe. *(New Sneakers for a New Age.)* I didn't stop until I'd built a tower of shoeboxes on the counter.

"Take a buyout?" the woman asked as she rang me up.

I nodded.

I gave her my credit card, and she handed me a bright purple pedometer. "On the house," she said. "It's the least Balancing Act can do for you."

"Thanks," I said. I hooked it onto my waistband, and that's when I started to walk.

DAY 2
54 steps

UGH.

DAY 3
28 steps

SO THIS IS ROCK BOTTOM.

DAY 4
17 steps

NO, THIS IS.

Keep reading! Buy The Wildwater Walking Club.

The Wildwater Walking Club: Back on Track (#2)

For Noreen, Tess, and Rosie, walking the beach together every day has been everything. But after all those steps forward, The Wildwater Walking Club is doing some serious backsliding. A new adventure might be just what they need. Their destination: Provence, the ultimate lavender trip. It turns into the trip of a lifetime, filled with Van Gogh and vineyards, wine and chocolate, plus lavender and more lavender. Join Noreen, Rosie and Tess as they get back on track!

Buy The Wildwater Walking Club: Back on Track (#2)

The Wildwater Walking Club: Step by Step (#3)

They thought they'd have their lives all figured out by now. But change is blowing in along with the crisp fall air, and they're finding out that life for 40-to-forever women is not for sissies. Hitting the road again might be just what The Wildwater Walking Club needs.

Buy The Wildwater Walking Club: Step by Step (#3).

Have You Read?

Never Too Late: Your Roadmap to Reinvention (without getting lost along the way)

Wondering how to get to that life you really thought you'd be living by now? Claire Cook shares everything she's learned on her own journey— from writing her first book in her minivan at 45, to walking the red carpet at the Hollywood premiere of *Must Love Dogs* at 50, to becoming an international bestselling author and a sought after reinvention speaker.

You'll hop on a plane with Claire as you figure out the road to your own reinvention: getting a plan, staying on track, pulling together a support system, building your platform in the age of social networking, dealing with the inevitable ups and downs, overcoming perfectionism, and tuning in to your authentic self to propel you toward your goals.

Time Flies

Two best friends. A high school reunion. And a rollicking road trip down memory lane.

Time Flies is an epic trip filled with fun, heartbreak and

friendship that explores what it takes to conquer your worst fears so you can start living your future.

Wallflower in Bloom

Deirdre Griffin has a great life. It's just not her own. She's the round-the-clock personal assistant to her charismatic, high-maintenance, New Age guru brother Tag. While drowning her sorrows in Tag's expensive vodka, she decides to use his massive online following to get herself voted on as a last-minute *Dancing with the Stars* replacement. Deirdre's fifteen minutes of fame have begun.

Seven Year Switch

Seven Year Switch is the story of a single mother whose husband ran off to join the Peace Corps, leaving her with a three-year-old. Seven years later, just when they've figured out how to make it on their own, he's ba-ack, proving he can't even run away reliably! Now Jill has to face the fact that there's simply no way she can be a good mom without letting her ex back into her daughter's life. They say that every seven years you become a completely new person, and it takes a Costa Rican getaway to help Jill make her choice—between the woman she is and the woman she wants to be.

Must Love Dogs, the series

Based on the bestselling novel-turned-romantic comedy movie starring Diane Lane and John Cusack!

Dogs, dating, adorable preschoolers, and meddling family in every book.

"Voluptuous, sensuous, alluring and fun. Barely 40 DWF seeks special man to share starlit nights. Must love dogs."

Must Love Dogs (#1)
Must Love Dogs: New Leash on Life (#2)
Must Love Dogs: Fetch You Later (#3)
Must Love Dogs: Bark & Roll Forever (#4)
Must Love Dogs: Who Let the Cats In? (#5)
Must Love Dogs: A Howliday Tail (#6)
Must Love Dogs: Hearts & Barks (#7)

Keep reading! Go to ClaireCook.com to find links to buy books.

Acknowledgments

I couldn't have written *Shine On* without all the fabulous midlife women who chimed in on Facebook, Twitter, in person, and via email to share their thoughts and dreams and stories with me. Thank you from the bottom of my heart for helping this book come alive and for teaching me so much along the way.

Another huge thank you to my awesome readers for reading my books, spreading the word, and continuing to give me the gift of my forty-to-forever career.

Many, many thanks to Jack Kramer, Ken Harvey and April Eberhardt for insightful, detailed feedback and much appreciated encouragement. Thanks to Beth Hoffman for an early impromptu chat that helped the pieces of this book begin to fall into place.

Thanks to Jake, Kaden and Garet for always being there when I need you. And to my cats for always making sure I get to work at the crack of dawn.

About Claire

I wrote my first novel in my minivan at 45. At 50, I walked the red carpet at the Hollywood premiere of the adaptation of my second novel, *Must Love Dogs*, starring Diane Lane and John Cusack, which is now a 7-book series.

I'm the *New York Times*, *USA Today*, and #1 Amazon bestselling author of 20 books. If you have a buried dream, take it from me, it is NEVER too late!

I was born in Virginia and lived for many years in Scituate, Massachusetts, an awesome beach town between Boston and Cape Cod. My husband and I now live on St. Simons Island, Georgia, a magical snowless place to walk the beach, ride our bikes, and make new friends.

I have the world's most fabulous readers and I'm forever

grateful to all of you for giving me the gift of my late-blooming career.

Shine On!

HANG OUT WITH ME:

ClaireCook.com
Facebook.com/ClaireCookauthorpage
Twitter.com/ClaireCookwrite
Instagram.com/ClaireCookwrite
Pinterest.com/ClaireCookwrite
BookBub.com/authors/claire-cook
Goodreads.com/ClaireCook
Linkedin.com/in/ClaireCookwrite

Be the first to find out when my next book comes out and stay in the loop for giveaways and insider extras: ClaireCook.com/newsletter/